STUDIES IN GERMAN LITERATURE,
LINGUISTICS, AND CULTURE

VOL. 17

STUDIES IN GERMAN LITERATURE, LINGUISTICS, AND CULTURE

VOL. 17

Editorial Board

CAMDEN HOUSE

Columbia, South Carolina

The Best Novellas of Medieval Germany

Konrad von Würzburg. Manessische Liederhandschrift, 383r,
University of Heidelberg, cpg. 848.

The Best Novellas of Medieval Germany
Translated with an Introduction

by J. W. Thomas

CAMDEN HOUSE

Set in Garamond type and printed on
acid-free Glatfelder paper.

Contents

Preface

The five novellas that have been selected here as being the best of medieval Germany date from about 1195 to about 1280, a period that includes the golden age of courtly literature and the first decades of its decline. They present a wide variety of content and reveal the most important characteristics of this literature: its heroism and fantasy, irony and humor, piety and didacticism. Since several of the works are quite controversial, notes have been added to point out some of the major questions that scholars have examined and a few of the different interpretations that have been advanced. However, no attempt has been made to give a full account of the scholarship involved, which includes hundreds of significant studies.

I believe that most of those who are familiar with Middle High German literature will agree that the novellas in this collection, with one possible exception, belong to the best of their time, if not actually to the top five. The questionable choice, *Laurin*, was included in part because of its lasting popularity and a feeling that medieval magic and Germanic heroes should be represented. *Poor Heinrich*, *Helmbrecht*, and short selections from *Laurin* have been previously translated. The other novellas appear here in English for the first time.

I wish to thank the Continuum Publishing Corporation for permission to use the translation of *Helmbrecht*, which is to appear in its *German Medieval Tales*, ed. Francis Gentry, The German Library, vol. 4.

J.W.T.
Lexington, Ky., May 1983.

Introduction

Poor Heinrich

THE AUTHOR OF *Poor Heinrich,* Hartmann von Aue, is mentioned in no historical document, and little is known of his life beyond that which he tells us at the beginning of his novella. Here he gives his name and says that he is an educated member of the servant nobility. Other sources indicate that he lived in the canton of Zurich, composed between 1180 and 1203, went on a crusade, and died sometime after 1210 and before 1220. Hartmann was the earliest and most versatile of the great writers of medieval Germany's classical period. His *Erec* and *Iwein* are the first Arthurian novels in the German language, his *Gregorius* is the outstanding medieval treatment of the church legend, and his songs belong to the best lyric poetry of the day.

In the introduction to his novella, Hartmann says that he is retelling a story that he found written. If this statement is factual and not merely a literary conceit, then his source has not survived, for no extant narrative composed before *Poor Heinrich* has the same plot and characters.[1] There are, however, two tales that were widely known in Hartmann's time which could have supplied the nucleus for his work: the account of Amicus and Amelius and the legend of the conversion of Emperor Constantine. In the first story Amelius cures the leprous Amicus by killing his own sons so that his friend can bathe in their blood. This devotion is at once rewarded when God restores the boys to life. In the legend Constantine's leprosy is to be treated in the same manner, but at the last moment he refuses to allow the children to be sacrificed. Later, while being baptized by Pope Sylvester, he is healed. It is quite possible that Hartmann had read some version of both of these narratives, perhaps in the same manuscript.

The most important developments that *Poor Heinrich* reveals with respect to the earlier stories are the addition of the Job theme and the substitution of a strong-willed heroine for the passive and helpless children.[2] The parallels between the character and experiences of Hartmann's hero and Job are consistent and appear throughout the novella. Their effect is two-fold: the miracle that cures the hero does not come as a surprise ending but is implicit in the beginning, and it is a reward not only for compassion but also for complete acceptance of God's will. The result is that *Poor Heinrich*, in spite of an improbable plot, displays a universality that is quite lacking in the various accounts of Amicus and Amelius and of the Sylvester legend.

Like the Book of Job, the German story begins with high praise of its hero as a man of great wealth and virtue. Indeed, Hartmann goes far beyond the Biblical account in his attempt to portray Heinrich as an exemplary character who possesses every desirable social and moral trait. The author apparently wishes to forestall any suspicion that the impending catastrophe is a punishment for an error or shortcoming. It does not strike him by chance, however, but by the express command of God. This is the first of a long series of divine interventions indicated by the narrator and (less reliably) by the characters, that permeate the novella and form its most significant motif.

The sudden reversal of Heinrich's fortunes, caused by his leprosy, elicits the first of the narrator's three direct comparisons of his hero and Job. The second comes soon afterwards when the nobleman's unrestrained grief is contrasted with the limitless patience that in sermon parables, though not in the Bible itself, is ascribed to Job. Nevertheless, the connection between the two stories has been established, and Hartmann's audience is prepared to mark the chain of events that will lead to the justification of the hero and his return to health and high position. This expectation is only confirmed by the physician's discouraging report, that the hero would never recover unless God himself wanted to be the doctor. Heinrich's belief that his leprosy is God's punishment for his ingratitude is not supported by the narrator and is no more than a rationale for his suffering. Job's friends also thought that great misfortune must be an evidence of sin.[3]

The affectionate relationship that develops between the nobleman and the farmer's daughter, the God-given kindly nature that is the source of her compassion for her lord, and the divinely inspired resolve to die for him are at once recognized as elements of a benevolent plan. And those familiar with the author's *Erec* might suspect that the girl's exceptional beauty would also play a role. In fact, the resolution of Heinrich's inner conflict at the crucial, dramatic moment involves purely human as well as Christian and Old Testament elements, for it is the sight of the beauty of the naked girl that awakens the compassion that leads to his resignation to the will of God. He therefore passes from aesthetics through morality to religion.[4]

Since the only indication of evil in Heinrich is his agreement—made when he was mortally ill—to the girl's sacrifice, the decision not to permit it should be considered a final rejection of temptation in the manner of Job rather than a conversion. However, Hartmann was too practical and too much a moralist to let all of the nobleman's suffering go for nothing. Like his other heroes and heroines,

Heinrich is improved by his experience as his former self-centered spirit is transformed into a new kindness. Later we learn that he served God better than before.

The farmer's daughter acts not only as an agent to arouse Heinrich's compassion and lead him to self-denial, but also as a contrast figure. She too is introduced with high praise: for her beauty and charm and especially for her kindly spirit. This kindness was the chief cause of her always being with her lord and was behind her decision to give her life to save him. However, she is a very impressionable child and is soon led astray by the arguments (borrowed from sermons) that she uses to persuade her parents to approve. She quickly becomes a religious fanatic who will have nothing to do with this world and cannot wait for death. Losing sight of her original goal, the healing of Heinrich, she is concerned only with the heavenly crown that her sacrifice will bring her. Thus, while Heinrich's way is taking him from egocentricity to compassion and a new kindness, hers goes from kindness to a zealot's complete preoccupation with self.[5]

The girl's martyr spirit is so overpowering that her parents and Heinrich consent to her death and the physician is convinced that no pain will cause her to weaken. Her mania well serves God's purpose, for it not only creates the situation that brings out Heinrich's compassion, but also provides him with a striking example of the willing renunciation of life and worldly pleasures. However, the girl too is soon in need of a cure. She is near death from the distress of having her sacrifice denied when He who sees the inmost heart intervenes. He had tested Heinrich and her as He had tested Job and, observing their basic faithfulness and compassion, now heals them both. They have a long and happy life before entering God's kingdom.

The story deals with the renunciation of self that leads people to God and to each other and with the proper balance between the enjoyment of this world's pleasures and the anticipation of the joys of heaven. This dual theme is supported by several motifs that run through the work. One, divine intervention in human affairs, has been discussed. Another is kindness, an attribute that is frequently mentioned—in connection with God, the girl, Heinrich, and the friends who welcome him home—and is the source of all the happy relationships. The several terms that refer to healing and health make up a third prominent motif, for the work is in essence the account of two people who become sick and are made whole.

Perhaps the most interesting motif is that of the bride. During his three years at the farm, the nobleman calls the little girl his bride; in her religious frenzy she looks forward to becoming the bride of Christ; her journey, in fine clothing, to Salerno is like a bridal journey, although we do not yet know who the groom will be; and at the end the peasant girl weds the nobleman, in a marriage that symbolically links the enjoyment of this world with the anticipation of heaven.

Hartmann concentrates on making his two main characters and their reactions plausible and is not concerned with further realism. The superstition that human blood would cure leprosy is a heathen one and the operation that was planned could never have been performed openly in Christian Italy. Moreover, patients were not completely stripped for any operation; only the part of the body to be treated was bared. And it is most unlikely that Heinrich's advisors, in the class-conscious High Middle Ages, would have counseled him to wed a commoner, free or not. The blood sacrifice, the nude girl, and the marriage of peasant and nobleman are fairy tale elements, and the author's audience would have recognized them as such.[6]

Like the other novellas of this collection, *Poor Heinrich* is composed in rhymed couplets of basically iambic tetrameter lines. The language is simple and clear, without being naive, and there are very few rhyme and verse fillers. Indeed, the verse itself is perhaps the best of medieval German narrative literature. Hartmann achieves his effects here, not by means of ornamentation and hyperbole, but by sharp contrasts and dramatic situations, such as that in which Heinrich hears the whetting of the knife and looks through the knothole at the beautiful, bound figure of the girl. The following scene reveals another trait of Hartmann, his occasional switch from serious drama to slapstick comedy. For the description of the naked, but unabashed, eleven-year-old girl sitting on the operating table and rudely berating the learned physician and the subdued nobleman was certainly intended to be humorous.

Hartmann's story has been relatively influential on modern German literature. It has been treated in a long ballad by Adelbert von Chamisso, in an opera by Hans Pfitzner, in a novella by Ricarda Huch, and in a drama by Gerhart Hauptmann. Rudolf Borchardt's version is the best known of many modern German translations. The tale also appears in American literature: in Longfellow's verse novel, *The Golden Legend*, for which it provides the basic framework. The text used for the translation is that by Hermann Paul and Ludwig Wolff.[7]

Moriz von Craûn

Since this novella is found only in a single, late manuscript, names no author, and is mentioned by no medieval writer, little is known about the circumstances of its composition. Rhyme studies of the extant version have indicated that the work was originally in one of the dialects of the region between Strassburg and Worms, while investigations of style and literary influences have produced estimated dates of composition that extend from 1180 to 1250. To these conclusions one can add only that the author was well read in the literature of his time, probably knew French, and wrote for a courtly audience.[8] The names of the chief characters of the novella are those of historical figures. The best known of several lords of Craon with the name Maurice was Maurice II, who died in 1190. If he was the one cast as the hero of the story, then the wife of his neighbor, Viscount

Richard de Beaumont, would have been the heroine. However, it is unlikely that the events described had any factual basis.[9]

Perhaps no other work of medieval German literature has been the object of such diverse evaluations and expositions as has *Moriz von Craûn*. It has been interpreted in many ways: as a model of courtly manners, a didactic poem, a loose collection of parodies, and an erotic anecdote, among others. Most studies, however, have avoided strict categories and emphasized its varied content or stressed its incongruities. Actually the work is a tightly organized and consistent satire of a favorite minnesong convention (the service of a lady for a lover's reward) and certain elements of courtly narrative literature (ostentatious extravagance, prodigal generosity, and success in tournaments) which were portrayed as prerequisites of knighthood.[10]

The relatively long introduction with its history of the varying fortunes of chivalry from the Trojan War to the Carolingian Empire and the subsequent discourse on courtly love set the stage for humorous satire. The readers (or listeners) are expected to remember that the conquests of Charlemagne were in the distant past at the beginning of the story proper and that the decline of Rome was symbolized by Nero's sexual aberrations, that were more revolting than this courtly love, but perhaps no more unnatural. It is also assumed that they will compare the tournament sport of which Moriz is so fond with Nero's use of armed force for entertainment on the one hand and the military exploits of such national heroes as Hector, Caesar, and Roland on the other. In short, the audience is expected to realize that the narrator's praise of the French chivalry of his day is ironic and that chivalry is actually in its third period of decline. The events that follow are to be judged and interpreted with this in mind.[11]

If the discussion of courtly love and its power indicates that the knights of Moriz's day lacked the virility of their predecessors, the lover's lament with which the hero describes his situation at once shows him to be no exception. This impression is heightened of course in the following scene when he is at first so affected by the lady's mere presence that he cannot speak and later is the butt of her jokes. The narrator can certainly expect the behavior here to be measured against the bearing and feats of the warriors of old.

The highly ornate ship with which Moriz begins his campaign to gain a lover's pay serves as a vivid and expressive symbol. It is a splendid, colorful facade, a make-believe warship with cloth bulkheads, a toy with no function commensurate with its great cost. As such it represents all of the empty pretense and ineffectiveness of chivalry as Moriz practices it: wasteful extravagance, combat which furthers no national ends, and generosity that neither satisfies the wants of the poor nor wins allies. The audience for whom the novella was composed was accustomed to interpreting symbols and would not have missed the connection between the fake ship and the fake chivalry. The ship's voyage across the peaceful fields might even have evoked a ludicrous comparison with the stormy voyages of Aeneas and his warriors, well known through Heinrich von Veldeke's account, which the author mentions.[12]

The hero arrives at the lady's castle, sets up his magnificent tent, opens a cask of fine wine, and prepares to receive guests. However those who come to enjoy his hospitality are not nobles but a swarm of vagrant entertainers, enough to carry away a house. To be sure, knights arrive in the morning: to eat and drink in quantities that, since they were about to participate in a tournament, were certainly excessive. This is perhaps the reason why the hero manages to unhorse so many in such a perfunctory manner. Even though he uses up more spears in a day than the inveterate jouster Ulrich von Liehtenstein did during his entire Venus journey and three times as many as the fabulous Gahmuret did at Kanvoleis, the account is amusingly routine. It is clear that the narrator has no intention of letting Moriz appear truly heroic.

Having presented extravagant display and mock warfare in a ridiculous light, the narrator now proceeds to expose lavish generosity, which in much courtly literature is portrayed as a special mark of chivalry. A beginning had been made in the story of Moriz's hospitality of the morning and the evening before (which hadn't turned out quite right). Then, during the tournament, he not only did not claim the steeds he had won from his fallen opponents, but even gave away his own horses, one after the other, as soon as they began to sweat from exertion. There was always someone at hand to take them. This liberality as well as his success in the tournament probably parodies similar behavior and events in Hartmann's *Erec*.

After the tournament Moriz offers his expensive ship to the pages who had assisted with the contest. However, as soon as they begin to dismantle it, the vagabonds again appear in countless numbers to strip and fight over it in a highly amusing episode. When everything is gone and the hero's attendants have fled to save their own belongings, a man comes and asks him for his hauberk, which Moriz removes and gives away. Then he sits down to take off his mail stockings to present to the next petitioner.

Since he has demonstrated his chivalry and served his lady by inordinate expenditures, unprecedented success in jousting, and boundless munificence, Moriz is now ready to receive his reward, and indeed a messenger from the lady appears to bid him come at once, just as he is, half dressed and unbathed. The hero is led to a splendid room that gleams like a cathedral and contains a wondrous bed of gold, ivory, and rare wood, covered by the finest cloth and furs. The lengthy description of the bed and the reference to a cathedral make it obvious that the narrator is again presenting an elegant symbol, that of the cult of courtly love.[13]

In the following series of dialogues—between the recalcitrant lady and her girl attendant, the girl and the knight, and again the lady and the girl—the preposterous arguments of the romantic maiden are the chief sources of humor and satire. In a bizarre twist of reasoning she maintains that the lady will lose her honor if people ever find out that she refused to go to bed with the knight and begs her in the name of God to do her duty. For his part, Moriz insists that the lady's husband, as a man of courtly manners, would command her to pay him properly for his service if he knew of the situation.

The drama that ensues when Moriz enters the lady's bedroom is slapstick comedy that evokes pertinent comparisons. The remorse of the husband at having accidentally killed a man and his falling in a faint on bumping his shin remind one that the men of modern chivalry have neither the mental nor the physical toughness of the heroes of the past, while the calculated action of the lady in yielding to Moriz as the best way out of an awkward situation contrasts sharply with the veiled and elusive eroticism of the minnesong. The bed in which she fulfills her pledge is, of course, not the fabulous bed of courtly love, but a marriage bed, that is defiled by an act of simple adultery from which all romanticism has been stripped. As Moriz gets up to leave, the narrator refers to him as a *wîgant,* a warrior of the heroic period, thus adding an ironic commentary on the deeds of the contemporary knights.

The last scene well illustrates the author's manipulation of traditional literary situations. The tableau is that of the type of early minnesong known as the *Frauenstrophe* or lady's stanza: forsaken and lonely the heroine stands by the window on a spring morning, looking out over the blooming roses and heather to the green forest while listening to the sweet singing of the birds; the many joys of nature recall her own sorrow, and she bemoans the loss of her lover. Like the lady of the songs, she is a sympathetic and poetic figure. However, when she expresses the hope that the God who blots out her sin will send the knight back to her, we remember that their relationship was an adulterous one that was not even based on affection, and all the pathos turns to humor.

Moriz von Craûn has a clearly defined five-part structure which resembles that of several courtly novels. After a rather lengthy introduction sets the stage, there comes a story inclosed in a framework. The latter consists of an initial section that presents the hero and a discourse by the narrator on courtly love and a final section focused on the heroine, who expounds on the same subject. In between are two sets of episodes. The ones associated with the ship ridicule by exaggeration certain traits that courtly epic verse connects with knightly behavior, while those linked to the bed form a burlesque of the lyric convention of the lover's pay.

Although the novella exposes folly, it is not didactic in the usual sense of the word, since the folly is not of real life, but only of literature. The story is simply a hilarious farce that lampoons popular literary conventions by presenting them in caricature, supporting them with ridiculous arguments, and emphasizing their incongruities. As the conceits of courtly writing were the objects of parody almost from the time of their first appearance in Germany, it is difficult to assess the influence that this novella may have had on subsequent humorous works with the same targets. At least one of these, however, the verse novel, *Service of Ladies* (1255), by Ulrich von Liehtenstein, is sufficiently similar to make a direct relationship probable.

Two texts were used for the translation, the Early New High German version of the manuscript and the Middle High German reconstruction by Ulrich Pretzel and his colleagues, who have presented both versions on facing pages in their edition. Most of the translation follows the reconstructed text, however all the verses that it omits have been restored.[14]

Heinrich von Kempten

Heinrich von Kempten was written by Konrad von Würzburg, one of the most facile and prolific authors of Middle High German literature. Historical records tell only that he died in 1287 in Basle, leaving behind a house, a wife, and two daughters. However, some additional biographical information can be gleaned from his works. These indicate that he was born between 1220 and 1230 in Würzburg of a middle-class family, had a good education, may have lived for a while in the lower Rhineland area of Germany, and spent the last two decades of his life in Basle as an independent author who supported himself by writing on commission for the nobility, higher clergy, and wealthy patricians of the city and the surrounding area. Attempts to determine a relative chronology of his works on the basis of their language and style have been inconclusive.

Konrad's novels, novellas, church legends, short stories, didactic verse, and minnesongs amount to some eighty-five thousand lines of narrative and lyric verse, all of which displays a high degree of technical proficiency. This can be seen especially in the incomparable virtuosity with which he plays with rhyme and meter in his songs: in some the complex patterns are so smoothly integrated that they almost escape attention, in others the poet ostentatiously flaunts his skill. Konrad's subjects are the traditional ones that had entertained the courtly audiences of Western Europe for half a century or more, and his chief sources were the popular works of French and Medieval Latin literature.

In spite of his considerable gifts, few of Konrad's writings can be ranked among the best of medieval literature. His songs suffer from a lack of originality and personal involvement, and his verse novels—which contain many fine scenes and episodes—reveal the author's inability to arrange material on a large scale around an idea, a character, or a situation in such a way that the parts form a unified whole. His particular talent shows itself to the greatest advantage in his short narratives, the most distinguishing characteristics of which are their historical settings, didactic tendencies, and exploitation of the incongruous and grotesque. *Heinrich von Kempten* shares these traits with the others, but with respect to its primary feature, the emphasis on humor, it stands alone among the verse tales as well as among the rest of Konrad's writings.[15]

The source of the novella, so says the author in the concluding verses, was a Latin work. Actually, there are two Latin versions of the story extant (at least one of which antedates Konrad's) and two more German versions. However, since his account is somewhat different from any of these and much longer, it is possible that the variant he used has been lost. In any case, he appears to have been also familiar with another work in which Emperor Otto plays a role, the popular verse novel *Duke Ernst* that was current in both German and Latin at the time when Konrad was writing. The novel not only reveals many detailed similarities to the novella with regard to plot and characters, but also describes the initial confrontation between the emperor and his vassal as an amusing, though bloody, episode. It may have been this scene that inspired the humor of Konrad's tale, for the other variants of *Heinrich von Kempten* present the corresponding scene in a less comical manner.[16]

The historical matter of the novella has been somewhat distorted, as is usually the case in medieval literature. The emperor is surely Otto the Great, although certain elements—the red beard, the tyrannical disposition, and the campaign in Apulia—were borrowed from his son Otto II. There is no documentary record of the episodes described or of a Heinrich von Kempten, but there was a well-known abbey at Kempten, founded by Charlemagne's wife Hildegard, of which the knight might have been a vassal. The choice of Bamberg as the location for the festival that introduces the story adds to the verisimilitude of the historical background, for it was an imperial city during Otto's reign.

Heinrich von Kempten is basically an extended amusing anecdote or *Schwank* in which there are two parallel comic scenes, rather than the usual one. The humor of the first episode stems from irony and incongruity. The irony is that the guileless boy who has come to Bamberg to learn courtly manners becomes a victim of and a witness to the crudest savagery, perpetrated by those who were to have been his teachers. The incongruity is evident in the juxtaposition of the Easter mass and the gory murder, the breaches of the class system as the steward attacks the duke's son and the knight assaults the emperor, and the unpredictable relationship of cause and effect when the trifling indiscretion of the boy initiates an escalation of violence to the point where the empire itself is threatened. The climax is the incomparable tableau which shows the mightiest of the German emperors, dressed in state, lying amid the food and dishes of the banquet, while the knight kneels on him and holds him fast by his prized beard. Otto's wry remarks about Heinrich's talents as a barber show that even he was impressed by the humor of the situation.

The matter of propriety, that in different forms is the source of the humor of the first episode, reappears in the second. Medieval literature is particularly concerned that clothing should properly reflect rank and character. Inappropriate dress is either tragic or comic, while nakedness (which wipes out class distinctions) is almost always amusing, especially when an attribute of a bold nobleman. The bathtub scenes of *Parzival, Tristan and Isolde,* and *Service of Ladies* are part of the standard comic repertoire of their times, while the nakedness of Iwein, Jeschute, Walther von der Vogelweide's *wunderwol gemachet wîp* (beautiful woman), and the heroes of the many tales of a nude monarch is the source of sophisticated as well as slapstick comedy. The facetious treatment of Hartmann's naked maiden and the half-dressed Moriz has been mentioned. Konrad's audience, accustomed to the splendid trappings of most knights in combat, would certainly have laughed appreciatively at the picture of the bare hero charging boldly into the fray. The humor that appears later, during the second meeting of knight and emperor, was of a different kind, one that stressed wit and dissimulation. It too was a favorite of medieval poets, especially the writers of short stories.[17]

The novella is carefully structured and presents a symmetrical pattern of similarities and contrasts in which parallel elements reinforce each other. The two episodes have the same basic plot. The hero appears on the scene as the advisor of a high-ranking Swabian nobleman (the boy, the abbot). The development toward a dramatic climax starts with an indiscretion (of the boy, of the emperor) that invites a cowardly attack (by the steward, by the citizens). Heinrich's loyalty and impetuousness cause him to intervene in an unorthodox manner and shed a great deal of blood, which leads to a confrontation with the emperor. The latter brings serious charges against the knight, who tries to excuse himself and gain Otto's pardon. These similarities underscore the chief differences between the two parts of the story, which lie in the settings and the conclusions.

The background of the first episode is the peaceful Easter festival, while that of the second is a military campaign, in which the hero is most reluctant to participate. Since the first ended in violence and estrangement, the perceptive reader or listener can expect the second to end in reconciliation. The symmetrical pattern is completed when the last paragraph of the story proper reveals a completely different side of the emperor's character from that presented in the first paragraph. The only significant motif of the story, Otto's beard, also contributes to the structural unity. It is mentioned four times in the first episode and twice in the second and stands as an amusing symbol of the emperor's anger and the knight's audacity.

The personalities of Otto and Heinrich are by no means stereotyped and add considerably to the charm of the story. The narrator's introductory comments prepare one for the emperor's tyrannical behavior, but his sense of humor comes as a surprise. His amusing comments at the conclusion of part one serve as a bridge to the gratitude, humor, and affection that he displays at the end of the story. The first unexpected trait of Heinrich's character appears in his vigorous protest against going to Italy, which shows him to be a cautious person when not in a rage; a second is seen in the practical and matter-of-course manner with which he returns to his bath after having done what he considered his duty. As a warrior he contrasts sharply and amusingly with the typical hero of courtly literature.

The brief epilogue is important not only because it establishes the authorship and source of the story, but also because it indicates an approximate date of composition and tells something about Konrad's clients and his manner of carrying out his commissions. The "Lord of Diersburg" appears to have been a certain Berthold, who held the position of provost from 1260 to about 1270. It is interesting that he, a prominent ecclesiastic, should have wanted a German version of an amusing anecdote, rather than a church legend, and that he should have brought the poet to Strassburg to compose the work, rather than send his valuable Latin manuscript to Basle. One wonders whether Konrad's high praise of his client was a spontaneous expression of his admiration or simply an implied part of the contract.

Konrad's popularity during the medieval period is seen in the relatively large number of extant manuscripts in which his works appear, the praise of his contemporaries and later writers, and his inclusion by the mastersingers among the twelve old masters. That *Heinrich von Kempten* in particular was well known is indicated by the fact that two later writers of amusing anecdotes tried to pass off their works as Konrad's. It is not unlikely that his novella was influential in establishing the humorous short narrative as a respectable literary form. The translation was made from the text of Edward Schröder.[18]

Laurin

Laurin belongs to the rather large number of thirteenth-century verse narratives that treat the heroic exploits of Dietrich of Verona (the historical Theodoric the Great) and his companions. The anonymous author of the novella is assumed to be a Tirolean, an itinerant singer and storyteller or perhaps a court poet, and the time of composition has been variously estimated from about 1170 to about 1250. Recent scholarship prefers the later date.[19]

Like *Heinrich von Kempten*, the work turns around two dramatic and violent episodes, constructed in parallel, that in effect cancel each other. These main episodes together with a short preface and a somewhat longer conclusion give it a four-part structure. Each section presents a sequence of light-heartedness, controversy or combat, and resolution of differences, which gives the account a consistent rhythm of increased and decreased tension. The setting is the early period of Dietrich's career—before the long, nonhistoric exile at Attila's court of which legend tells—and the characters, except for Laurin and Kühnhilde, are heroes who were so well known to the High Middle Ages that the author did not consider it necessary to introduce them. Indeed, Wieland's son Witege, Dietleib, Wolfhart, and the old Hildebrand all appear in other works of the Dietrich cycle.[20]

The theme of the story, the struggle between the two great warriors, Dietrich and Laurin, is presented at once in the preface, which praises first one and then the other, raises the question as to who is the mightier, and brings up the rose garden as a means of initiating a confrontation. In this scene the contrast of moods is not extreme, but is nevertheless perceptible: Witege's joyous eulogy of Dietrich leads to an acrimonious exchange between the latter and Hildebrand, which is resolved when Dietrich states that he will seek out Laurin.

The next section starts at the rose garden that "drove away all sadness," where "the warriors sat on the grass and forgot their troubles." This tranquility is shattered by the arrival of the angry dwarf and his victory over Witege. When Dietrich comes to the latter's aid, the main conflict begins, and takes unexpected turns as Dietrich reacts successively to Laurin's invincibility on horseback, impenetrable armor, magic cloak, and magic belt. Dietleib intervenes to rescue the dwarf, and Hildebrand finally makes peace among all parties.

Part three has a similar sequence of events, but here everything is on a much larger scale. In place of the rose garden there is the delightful meadow in front of the mountain—filled with flowers, birds, and tame animals—and the extravagant festival inside. On the renewal of hostilities, there is once more a preliminary struggle as Dietleib holds off the hordes of dwarfs while his companions arm. Again Dietrich comes to the aid of a friend in the nick of time, and a massive struggle ensues, whose course changes when the two men are joined by Hildebrand and then by Witege and Wolfhart and the giants rush in to help the dwarfs. Once more magic plays an important role. After Laurin is defeated a second time, he is saved by the intercession of Kühnhilde and Dietleib, who are supported by Hildebrand.

The purpose of this section is not only to portray greater joys and violence, but also to even the score between Laurin and Dietrich. The latter was certainly an accessory to the wanton destruction of the rose garden, and the sympathies of the listeners at the end of part two would probably have been with the dwarf. However, when Laurin breaks his word and imprisons his guests, the lord of Verona regains the audience's approval.

The last episode takes place back at Dietrich's court and is introduced by another large celebration. It is followed by a second petition of Kühnhilde in favor of Laurin and by counsel from Hildebrand as to how it should be granted. Then a final conflict arises as the dwarf refuses to be baptized. By the time he changes his mind, the poor treatment he has received from the youths at court and his great sorrow at losing Kühnhilde have so redeemed him with the audience that it welcomes his pardon and reconciliation with Dietrich. The conclusion thus preserves and completes a symmetrical structural pattern, a device by means of which the medieval poet made events predictable and therefore logical.

The driving force throughout most of the story is revenge. This motif first appears in the preface, where Hildebrand tells how Laurin avenges himself on those who harm his garden, and again when the dwarf does indeed try to get revenge by taking a hand and a foot from the two intruders. When Dietrich conquers him the lord of Verona declares that he will kill the dwarf to avenge his companion's humiliation and his own narrow escape. Later the dwarf's pride drives him to get revenge for his defeat, and Dietrich determines to destroy the entire race of dwarfs because of Laurin's treachery.[21]

A second and related motif is formed by the frequent forebodings that the narrator interjects between the arrival of Dietrich at the rose garden and the final defeat of Laurin. However, although these veiled predictions have an ominous sound and are calculated to heighten the suspense, they hint at danger, rather than doom, and do not create the heavy atmosphere of inexorable fate that the forebodings of the *Nibelungenlied* produce.

The most distinctive and most frequently occurring motif is the counsel motif. Every constructive action is the result of a specific recommendation. This usually comes from the wise Hildebrand, who guides his companions step by step, but others also advise. Dietrich warns Witege not to underestimate Laurin; Kühnhilde asks her brother's advice as to whether she should stay with the dwarf; Laurin asks her what he should do about the injury he has suffered; she counsels Dietleib on how to fight the dwarf; Laurin wants Ilsung to tell him how to become a Christian; and Dietrich requests the recommendation of his vassals concerning a name for Laurin. Because of all the advice, most of the action appears in duplicate: as counseled and as executed. These three motifs, like the symmetrical plot, contribute to the unity of the novella.

Laurin is less successful when it comes to presenting a uniform system of manners. It resembles other works of the Dietrich cycle in being strongly influenced by Arthurian literature and does not do as well as some in reconciling its courtly customs and conceits with heroic characters and motifs. Dietrich's decision to enhance his fame through single combat with Laurin is a stock element of the knightly tradition, but the uncontrollable fury with which he beats his helpless opponent against the ground and attacks a nobleman who tries to save him is clearly that of the Germanic berserker. The splendor and merry festivities inside the mountain are of the material with which Arthurian novels regaled their audiences, but the subsequent massacre which leaves the warriors wading in blood is not. The attitude of both Laurin and Dietrich toward Kühnhilde is that of the knight toward the highborn lady and reveals the courtly side of their natures: their fierce preoccupation with revenge shows the heroic side.[22]

A similar carelessness or naiveté of composition can be seen in *Laurin's* language and versification. Unlike the other novellas of this collection, it has frequent reiterations of the same words, rhymes, and formulas and a large number of obvious line and rhyme fillers. However the expression of the narrator, although repetitious, is always direct and animated, and the dialogue is natural and dramatic. Moreover, he is capable of rather subtle artistry. For example, when Laurin rides up to his red and gold garden, his weapons, armor, and riding gear all are gleaming with red and gold, so that he appears to be not just the defender, but also the very spirit, of the garden.

One of the most popular areas of scholarly activity with respect to *Laurin* has to do with possible sources, especially for the rose garden episode, to which many mythological and legendary analogues have been compared. The most promising of these is a folk tale of the Fassa Valley, which is below the Rose Garden massif of the Italian Tirol. It tells of a king who long ago lived high in the mountains and had beautiful meadows and gardens with roses much larger and redder than those of the present. One day strange warriors came and destroyed the roses, and when the king tried to drive them off, he was captured and taken away to their land. There he was forced to dance to entertain them in the evenings until at last he managed to escape and return home. Thinking that it had been the redness of his Alpine roses that had attracted the strangers, he placed a charm on them so that they could not be seen either by day or by night. But he forgot about the twilight, and then they gleamed as if the heights were on fire.

There are two plausible reasons for believing that this bit of folklore may have been a source for *Laurin*. The first is that it appears to be the attempt of a primitive society to explain a common natural phenomenon—the effect of the evening sun on the gray limestone of the Dolomites—and as such might well go far back beyond the thirteenth century. The second is that Laurin's shabby treatment in Verona does not quite fit the story and could have been taken over as a peripheral feature of more relevant material, such as that concerning the rose garden. The name of the Rose Garden massif is not necessarily significant since its age is unknown and it therefore might have been borrowed from *Laurin*.[23]

Whether or not there was a mythological or legendary source for the rose garden episode, one can be sure that there was a literary source, for its similarity to the opening scene and the Kalogrenant adventure of Hartmann von Aue's *Iwein* is too close for coincidence. There are even verbal echoes of the older work. It is likely that the author of *Laurin* was also familiar with Hartmann's *Erec*, which has a beautiful park with a fierce defender, a mighty dwarf king who forces the reluctant hero to fight him, and an unusual steed with trappings that remind one of Laurin's armor and riding gear.

The large number of extant manuscripts and early printings, the two continuations by later medieval poets, and the subsequent appearance of Low German, Danish, Faroese, and Czech versions indicate that *Laurin* may have been the most popular of the novellas of the German Middle Ages. It had such an effect on folklore that by the sixteenth century the dwarf king was thought to have been a historical figure. The story also left its mark on formal literature: on *Der Rosengarten zu Worms, Wolfdietrich von Salnecke*, and perhaps *Goldemar*. In addition, the description of the splendor and festivities inside the mountain and the reference to the swift passage of time there may have contributed to the legend of the Venus Mountain. A large fifteenth-century mural in the ruins of the Lichtenberg Castle in Tirol witnesses to the continued popularity of the story.[24]

Even in modern times it has not been completely forgotten by nonacademicians. Gerhart Hauptmann begins his long poem, "Die blaue Blume," with a reference to Laurin's rose garden, and Peter Hacks presents a new version of the novella with his "Geschichte vom König Laurin." The translation was made from the text by Karl Möllenhoff.[25]

Helmbrecht

The Wernher the Gardener who identifies himself in *Helmbrecht* as the author is linked to no other piece of literature, appears in no official document, and is mentioned by none of his contemporaries. The language of the two extant manuscripts and the geographical references in the work suggest that he was a Bavarian or Austrian, and certain literary relationships indicate that he composed his novella at some time between 1237 and 1290, but there is no convincing evidence with regard to his class or residence. It is most unlikely that Wernher actually was a gardener—similar symbolic titles were assumed by many thirteenth-century poets—and the various personal references he makes in *Helmbrecht* do not go beyond the conventional literary conceits of the period. Scholarly opinions therefore differ as to whether he was of peasant, bourgeois, or noble origin, was a cleric or a layman, was a homeless wanderer or a settled member of a community.

Whatever the author's particular situation may have been, it probably was less important for the story than were the general social conditions of his period, which form the background for *Helmbrecht*. In one manuscript the place names point to a setting in the border area of Bavaria and Austria, in the other they indicate a locale in the Austrian Traungau district. Both regions, like much of central Europe, were greatly affected by the social and economic changes that were occurring at this time. The shift in compensation for land use from payment in labor to payment in money generally favored the peasants and enabled some of them to become relatively wealthy, which tended to diminish the class distinctions between them and the minor nobility.[26]

The development of industry in the towns also improved the position of the peasants, since it was now possible for them to flee from the land and find employment as artisans. In some cases they even joined the retinues of the upper nobility as professional soldiers, thus taking positions that formerly were held by landless noblemen. The rise in the status of many peasants was occasionally marked by their giving up the clothing that custom, and sometimes law, had assigned them and wearing the dress of the upper classes at festive events, which no doubt antagonized those members of the poorer aristocracy who felt threatened by the social changes.

The decline of the feudal system in Germany and Austria was accompanied by a decline in the power of the central authority and an increase in lawlessness and political disorder. The death of Duke Friedrich II in 1246 and Emperor Friedrich II four years later left Austria and much of Germany without strong leadership. As a result there was little effective force to control the petty feuds of the minor noblemen, which were usually limited to raids on each other's unfortified villages, or to protect the merchants on the highways from the attacks of the so-called robber knights.[27]

The story that was placed in this setting of social change drew freely from other works. There is no indication that Wernher had a formal education, but he was at least familiar with the popular literature of the day. He refers to the tales of Troy and Charlemagne, both of which were available in German; the deaths of Dietrich's brother and Attila's sons at the hand of Wittig (the Witege of *Laurin*) in *The Battle of Ravenna;* the King Arthur material; *Duke Ernst;* and the songs of Neidhart von Reuenthal. Much of the adornment of young Helmbrecht's cap was borrowed from the splendid saddle in Hartmann's *Erec,* which also supplied the model for the comic flight of the wedding guests, while the first two dialogues between father and son appear to have been influenced by a similar discussion between the abbot and the hero in Hartmann's *Gregorius.* The passage in which the father compares the courtiers of former years with those of the present may have echoed similar social criticism in "Die Klage" (The Lament), a long didactic poem by Wernher's contemporary The Stricker. Other influences of German literature and Bible stories on *Helmbrecht* have been pointed out, but most of them are either of dubious validity or unimportant.[28]

The most significant contribution to Wernher's novella was made by Neidhart, who supplied the nucleus of the plot and its chief symbol, models for the ambitious and pretentious peasants, and an appropriate structure. One of Neidhart's amusing winter songs tells of a vain young peasant who wore his curly, blond hair long (like a nobleman) and had a splendid cap on which birds had been carefully embroidered with silk. He wanted to be considered the equal of the lesser courtiers, but, if they catch him—says the narrator—they will tear his cap to pieces so quickly that he will think the birds have flown away. Other winter songs tell of presumptuous and violent youths who imitate noblemen not only with their elegant clothing, but also by wearing swords and helmets. The source of the Gotelind episode is perhaps the summer song that tells of a peasant girl who refuses the suit of a farmer because she is determined to marry a knight; and the model for the mother who, according to her children, had had affairs with noblemen may have been Neidhart's older peasant woman who chased after his knightly narrator.[29]

Helmbrecht is unique among medieval novellas in that it consists basically of a series of dialogues, which take up about two-thirds of the verses and tell the story in full without relying on the narrative framework. The remaining one-third, with the exception of the introductory description of the hero's clothing, does little more than link the dialogues, bring in tangential material (the two feasts), and provide a somewhat perfunctory account of the fulfillment of the prophesies given in one of the dialogues.

This unusual structure was borrowed from Neidhart's summer songs. Typically these begin with a greeting to a semi-personified May who has arrived in all his fine raiment accompanied by the songs of many birds. The nature introduction is then often followed by an extended argument between a mother and a daughter as to whether the latter should put on her best clothing and go to meet a certain knight at a dance. The mother tells the daughter to remain in her station and warns her of the unhappy consequences of such social climbing, but in vain. We are not specifically informed that the mother's dire predictions are realized, however, we assume that they are. Wernher's chief adaptation of this basic pattern is the replacement of the girl with one of Neidhart's arrogant peasant youths. This causes the dialogue to become a father-son argument and leads to the substitution of a violent ending for the seduction and abandonment implied in the summer songs.

The single dialogue of the summer songs is expanded in *Helmbrecht* to a series of six conversations that take place at the family farm and are divided into three groups by the two departures of the hero. This arrangement shows a superficial similarity to the departure and return structure of the Arthurian novel as well as to a once-repeated prodigal son story, which may have added certain ironic and symbolic overtones to the narrative. However the form of the novella would have reminded the medieval listener first of all of the very popular summer songs of Neidhart and his many imitators. The splendidly dressed peasant with the birds on his cap and the heated discussions of parent and offspring would have recalled the incarnated May and the mother's attempt to restrain her socially ambitious daughter. These associations are important, for they set the stage for a satirical and humorous, rather than a tragic, story and thus reinforce the impression of incongruity and grotesqueness that is so characteristic of *Helmbrecht*.

Perhaps because the work consists primarily of dialogue, its plot appears to be less closely knit than those of many medieval novellas. However it is not without unifying elements. Among them are such parallel events as the peasant feast and the mock-courtly feast, the two homecomings, and the account of the dreams and their realization.

The function of the cap is especially significant. Since the dance scene depicted on it reappears in almost the exact center of the work and the cap itself at the end, it and all it symbolizes effectively tie together the beginning, middle, and conclusion. The merry nun who made the cap also contributes to the unity of the story in that her fate foreshadows that of Helmbrecht and Gotelind, whose vanity also led them to forsake their station in life.[30]

The figures which Wernher took over from Neidhart were type characters who possessed just those traits that would make them seem ludicrous to the latter's aristocratic audience. However during the process of epic expansion they acquired attributes not evident in the songs. The mother was certainly foolish, overly ambitious, and as a young woman had perhaps been inclined to welcome the amatory advances of noblemen. Still she was generous enough to sacrifice not only her cheese and eggs, but even her own clothing to outfit her son, and she treated him with compassion after he had been condemned and rejected by society. Gotelind, although displaying a comical greed when wooed by Lemberslint, was also unselfish toward her brother and, as far as we learn, did not reproach him for his part in her downfall. Helmbrecht himself reveals few, if any, virtues, but is nevertheless portrayed primarily as a foolish, misguided youth, rather than as a confirmed criminal, as a fitting object of laughter and ridicule, rather than of wrath. The author encourages us to feel sorry for him at the end.

The attitude of the author toward the father at first appears equivocal. When the latter supports the rigid class system, praises the mission of the farmer, advocates nobility of spirit, and declaims against the decay of courtly manners, he might be seen as a spokesman for Wernher, but when he pays more than three times as much as a horse is worth, admits ignorance concerning a bohort, and refuses to feed a stranger, he fits the stereotype of the stupid, uncouth, and stingy peasant of the popular dance songs and verse tales. At the end the elder Helmbrecht is revealed to be both mean and cowardly. Even though he supplied the horse that started his son on a life of crime (knowing full well the use to which it would be put), he not only refuses to help him, but cruelly taunts him and even strikes the innocent boy who leads him. The reason is clear. The last dream has not yet been fulfilled, and he does not want to be sheltering the blind cripple when his neighbors come to hang him. One wonders whether the author intended to imply that it was merely cowardice that made the farmer such a staunch supporter of the status quo. It is noteworthy that Gotelind, whose fault was much less than her brother's, does not turn to the father in her hour of need.[31]

Even though the narrator shows flashes of sympathy for his characters, his prevailing attitude toward them is that of the detached humorist. Humor indeed plays a consistent and largely self-sufficient role throughout most of the novella. Much of what Helmbrecht and his sister say is comic in its absurdity or pretentiousness, and the father's sermons often are amusingly inconsistent with his gift of a horse to one who intends to become a robber. The humor is even more pronounced outside of the long dialogues. A tone of ludicrous incongruity is established at the very beginning by the long description of the rude peasant in fine clothing; there is fine slapstick comedy in the scene where the homecoming

Helmbrecht, having tried to impress his family with his courtly sophistication, has to prove himself a true peasant in order to gain food and lodging; and the parody of the Arthurian marriage feast with its burlesque wedding and caricatures of great knights is amusing not only for its own absurdity, but also for the way it pokes fun at a favorite literary extravaganza.

The macabre humor of the latter part of the novella is somewhat different. It first appears when Helmbrecht recommends Gotelind as a wife for Lemberslint and tells his friend how she will care for him if he is maimed, blinded, or hung. The narrator's facetious suggestion that Gotelind's marriage may have been consummated by the sheriff's deputies is in the same vein, as are also the bold declarations of the cowardly farmers who unite to attack the blind cripple. The narrator provides the best example of such humor when he pretends horror at the merciless destruction of the cap while reporting the hanging of its owner in a most casual manner.[32]

Wernher's narrator, like most of his kind, is basically a comic figure who has his own role to play and cannot be trusted to speak for the author. One is therefore inclined to assume that the somewhat irrelevant warning at the end is also humor—a waggish threat directed at the immediate audience—especially since the narrator adds that it was actually he himself who had brought Helmbrecht to justice, that the story was in fact his own creation.

Despite the prevalence of humor in *Helmbrecht*, one should not assume that it is only a comical story. The crimes and the punishment of the hero were no more amusing in Wernher's day than now, and their treatment certainly indicates that the author had a serious purpose. Like many other thirteenth-century writers he was deeply concerned with what appeared to be the deterioration of the entire culture, and he directed his satire at every convenient target. The account of the runaway nun is probably a criticism of the clergy; the bleak portrait of contemporary courtly manners in the third dialogue is certainly an indictment of some of the courts; with young Helmbrecht's absurd report of the personal injuries he intended to avenge Wernher ridiculed the justifications for the feuds between neighboring knights; and the references to the corrupt judge and the rape of Gotelind make up a censure of the judiciary. The chief target of Wernher's satire, however, is the lack of stability in the class system, an evil, so he may have thought, that was largely responsible for all the others.

Although the laws that bound the peasant to the soil were not consistently enforced in Wernher's time, it was still widely assumed by clergy and laymen that one's station in life was divinely ordained and that the attempt to rise above it was a rejection of the divine order. The author implies that this sin of the young Helmbrecht led logically and inevitably to his outrages against society, especially against that class to which he had belonged. The rejection of his appointed station was also a repudiation of that of his father and was therefore the initial step in his violation of the Fourth Commandment, a transgression for which he was punished when he was sentenced for his civil crimes.[33]

In his attempt to show that Helmbrecht's mutilation and death were predetermined by the youth's unwillingness to remain a peasant, the author relies on two devices, one pointing forward, the other pointing backwards. The former is made up of the father's dreams, which constitute not only a prophesy but a leitmotif, since the theme of mutilation, blinding, and hanging reappears in the two following dialogues and is reenforced during the wedding feast by the dark forebodings of Gotelind. The latter is the splendid cap, whose destruction at the end reminds the reader that it was the first sign of the vanity and presumption that led the foolish youth astray. The object which had initially marked the hero as a comic figure is therefore ultimately seen as a symbol of that which caused his tragic death. A third motif that in retrospect lends an air of inevitability to the story is the soil. Helmbrecht renounces his calling as a tiller of the soil when he leaves home but is not welcomed on his return until he identifies himself as a plowman. At his death he receives a bit of earth instead of a wafer, "to help him against hell's fire;" however, his divorce from the soil is final, for instead of being buried, he is left to hang in a tree until the birds of the air have devoured him.

Wernher's work appears to have been fairly well known in the late medieval period. The Arthurian novel *Meleranz* by The Pleier has a passage dealing with the fall of Troy that is close enough to one in *Helmbrecht* to suggest that the author knew the novella. There are also verbal echoes in the satiric poems by the writer with the pseudonym Seifrid Helbling, enough to indicate rather liberal borrowing from Wernher. Direct references occur in the *Rhyme Chronicle* of Ottokar of Styria, who mentions the teaching of the elder Helmbrecht in a polemic against the use of peasants as troops, and in the writings of the Czech Thomas of Stitny, who uses the name of the hero as a common noun with the meaning "suitor."

Helmbrecht has not only been popular in recent times, but also influential. There are numerous translations (in Dutch, English, French, and New High German), and by 1950 the plot had been used by sixteen literary works and one opera. This translation was made from the text edited by Friedrich Panzer.[34]

Hartmann von Aue. Manessische Liederhandschrift, 184r,
University of Heidelberg, cpg. 848.

Poor Heinrich

A KNIGHT CALLED HARTMANN, who was a vassal of the Lords of Aue, was so learned that he could read whatever was written in books. He often looked into different ones, searching for something that would make troublesome hours more pleasant and was of such a nature as to endear him to men and honor God. He will now begin to tell you a story he found written. He gave his name in order to be rewarded for the pains he has taken with it and so that whoever reads it or hears it told after his death might pray to God for the welfare of his soul. They say that he who intercedes for others is his own messenger too and thereby redeems himself.

The knight read this tale about a nobleman, whose home was in Swabia, who lacked no virtue a young knight should have in order to gain the highest renown. No one in all the lands was so admired. He had noble birth, wealth, and many fine traits. As irreproachable as his origins were—equal to those of monarchs—and great his wealth, he was not nearly as rich in birth and possessions as in honor and spirit.

He was Sir Heinrich von Aue, a name well known. His heart had forsworn all deceit and rude manners, and it kept this oath steadfastly to the end so that his repute and life remained without blemish. He had all the worldly fame one could wish for, and with his many splendid qualities, could easily add to it. He was a flower of youth, a bright mirror of earthly joy, a diamond of constant loyalty, and a true crown of courtesy. He was a refuge for the oppressed, a shield for his clan, and an even scale of generosity that gave neither too much nor too little. He bore on his shoulders the heavy load of honor, was a bridge of counsel, could sing well of courtly love, and was mannerly and wise. He therefore was able to win the world's praise.

While Sir Heinrich was thus enjoying fame, wealth, a blithe spirit, and worldly pleasure—he was acclaimed and honored above all his kindred—his high self-esteem vanished as his station became very humble. With him it was seen, as also with Absalom, that the vain crown of worldly pleasure can fall from its greatest splendor into the dust. So the Scripture has told us. In one place it says there: "media vita in morte sumus," which means that, when we fancy we are living better than ever before, we are on the brink of death. The firmness of this world, its constancy, and its greatest might are powerless. We can see a true picture of that with the candle, which turns to ashes as it gives off light. We are of frail substance: look how our laughter is quenched by tears. Our sweetness is mixed with bitter gall: our blossom must fall just when it thinks itself most fresh.

It became clear in Heinrich's case that he who is most highly esteemed in this world is of little moment before God. At God's command he fell from his position of great honor to one of abased sorrow, for he became leprous. He was loathsome to men and women when they saw the grievous chastisement of God on his body. See how pleasing he was to the world before, and now he became so odious that no one wanted to look at him. So too it was with the noble and rich Job, who, in the midst of his happiness, was consigned in misery to the dunghill.

When poor Heinrich realized that he, like all thus afflicted, was offensive to everyone, his bitter grief parted him from Job's patience. For the good Job suffered with a calm spirit when he had to endure distress—illness and the world's scorn—for the welfare of his soul: he thanked God for it and was happy. Unfortunately, poor Heinrich did nothing of the kind; he was sad and depressed. His soaring heart ceased to fly, his swimming joy drowned, his pride fell, his honey became gall. A mighty, fierce thunderclap destroyed his midday as a heavy, dark cloud covered the gleam of his sun. He was sorely grieved that he had to leave behind so many honors and often cursed the day he was born.

Heinrich nevertheless was still a little comforted because he had often heard that there were many forms of the disease and that some were curable. He therefore harbored all kinds of views and hopes. He thought he could perhaps be healed and, on the advice of doctors, journeyed hastily to Montpellier. There he was quickly disillusioned, for he learned that he would never be free of his malady.

He heard this with regret and, travelling to Salerno, sought out there also the knowledge of the wise doctors for his healing. The best master he found at once told him something strange, that he could be cured but would forever remain uncured. "How can that be?" exclaimed Heinrich. "What you say is impossible. If I can be healed, I shall be healed, for I expect to do whatever is prescribed for me, regardless of the hardship or the cost."

"You might as well give up that hope," replied the master. "Your illness is such that a certain remedy can cure you, but it is useless for me to tell you that, since no one is so rich or clever that he can get it. You will therefore never recover unless God Himself wants to be the doctor."

"Why do you discourage me?" asked poor Heinrich. "I have great wealth. If you will do your duty, apply your skill, and not refuse my silver and gold, I'll make you so well disposed toward me that you will be very glad to heal me."

"I would most willingly serve you," said the master, "and if the remedy were of a kind that one could buy or obtain in any way, I would not let you perish. Unfortunately, that is not the case, and therefore my help must be denied you. You would have to produce a maiden of marriageable age who is willing to die for you. Now it is not human nature for one to do that gladly. Nothing else will work, only the heart's blood of a maiden: that would heal your leprosy."

Now poor Heinrich saw that it was not possible for one to find a person who would want to die for him. The faith that had brought him there was thus taken away, and from then on he no longer hoped to recover. So deep was his sorrow that he was greatly annoyed to have to go on living. He journeyed home and began to dispose of his landed property as well as his other wealth in the best manner possible, according to his own desires and the advice of wise counselors. With prudence he made his poor kinsmen rich and also comforted needy strangers so that God might be pleased to have mercy on his soul. He gave the remainder to cloisters. He thus parted with all his many possessions except for a farm in a clearing, to which he fled from society. This pitiable fate was lamented not just by him alone, because the people in all the lands where he was known grieved for him, and also those in foreign lands who knew him by report.

The free farmer who had always worked this tract never suffered the hardships endured by other farmers who had harsher lords and were spared neither taxes nor fees. His lord not only was satisfied with whatever the farmer gave willingly but also protected him from the oppression of others, so that no one in the country of his station was so prosperous. When poor Heinrich went to stay with him, he was well repaid and profited greatly for having spared the farmer, since the man was not annoyed at anything that happened because of him. He was loyal, willing to endure the burden and trouble of his presence, and took good care of him.

God had given the farmer a happy life for one in his position. He was able-bodied and had an upright wife and handsome children, which are indeed a true joy to a man. Among them, it is said, was a girl of eight years whose manner was very kind. She never wanted to move a foot's distance from her lord and, to gain his favor and a friendly word, served him in every way with loving attention. Moreover, she was so charming and beautiful that she would have been a suitable daughter for the emperor.

The others were inclined to avoid him to a certain extent, but she hurried to him at all times and never elsewhere. She was his only pleasure. With a child's unrestrained kindness, her heart was so turned to her lord that she was always at his feet, caring for him with charming zeal. He for his part also made her happy with whatever he could, giving her many of such things as were suitable for a child's play. Since children adapt easily, it was not hard to please her. He got her everything a child might like that was for sale—mirrors, hair ribbons, belts, and rings—and his favors made her feel so much at ease with him that he called her his bride. The sweet maiden never left him; to her he seemed without fault or blemish. This was partly the result of the childish gifts, but was much more because of the kindly nature that God had given her. She waited on him very tenderly.

Once when poor Heinrich had lived there for three years, God was afflicting him with great pain. The farmer, his wife, and their daughter—the maiden of whom I have told you—were then sitting with him at their work and lamenting their lord's distress. They had good reason to grieve because they feared that his death could harm them greatly and rob them of all esteem and property and that a new lord would be more severe. They kept thinking about this until the farmer began to speak as follows. "My dear lord," he said, "if you don't mind, I would like to ask a question: since there are so many masters of medicine in Salerno, how is it that no one's knowledge was able to cure your illness? Sir, that surprises me."

With bitter pain poor Heinrich then heaved a sigh from the depths of his heart that almost caused words to fail him: such was his regret. "I have well deserved this shameful humiliation from God," he said, "for you yourself have seen that my gate formerly was wide open to worldly pleasure and that no one ever had his own way among his kinsmen more than I. This could not be, because I did everything I wished. I paid little heed to Him whose grace had given me such a happy life, for my heart was then like that of all fools who think they can have esteem and riches without God's help. My foolish fancy deceived me because I had little regard for Him by whose grace much honor and wealth was mine. When the high gatekeeper lost patience with this pride, He closed the portals of bliss before me, and I shall never come in. My foolish wit has cost me that.

"God has punished me with a sickness from which no one can set me free. The exalted pay no attention to me, and the petty scorn me. However base he may be who catches sight of me, I must be even more worthless; he shows me his disdain by turning his eyes away. Your loyalty is now seen in your actions in letting me, a sick man, stay with you and not fleeing from me. Although your welfare greatly depends on me, you could nevertheless easily become reconciled to my death. Did ever a man in this world become more worthless and miserable? I, who was your lord, am now in need of your aid. My dear friend, you, your wife, and my little bride are earning eternal life by allowing me, sick as I am, to remain with you.

"I'll gladly answer your question. I could find no master in Salerno who wished or dared to take me as a patient, for the remedy with which I could recover from my sickness is something that no one in the world can possibly get. I was told nothing less than that I would have to find a maiden of marriageable age who was willing to suffer death for me. She would be cut open to the heart, for only her heart's blood could help me. Now it is quite impossible that anyone would want to die for me, and therefore I must endure shameful misery to the end. May God send it soon!"

That which he told the father was heard by the innocent maiden who was holding the feet of her beloved lord in her lap: one could well compare her childlike spirit to the kindness of angels. She noted carefully what he said and kept it in her heart until she went to bed that night. Then, while lying as usual at the feet of her father and mother—both of whom had gone to sleep—she breathed many deep sighs. Her grief at the lord's distress became so great that a rain of tears wet the feet of the sleepers and woke them.

When they felt the tears, they asked what had happened to her and what sort of trouble she was thus lamenting secretly. She didn't want to say, but after her father repeatedly threatened her and ordered that she tell them, she spoke, "You should be grieving with me. What can distress us more than that we are to lose our lord, and with him both property and esteem. We shall never get such a good one, who will treat us as he does."

"You are right, daughter," they said, "however giving way to grief and regret will not help us a bit. So stop this, dear child. We are as sorry as you, but cannot help him. God has taken him from us: we would curse anyone else who did it." Thus they quieted her, yet she remained sad that night and all the next day. Whatever anyone else did, her heart was still troubled when they went to bed as usual the following night. As soon as they had lain down at their accustomed place, she again prepared a bath of tears, for hidden in her heart was the greatest kindness I ever heard of in a child. What other one would have acted so? She decided that, if she lived until morning, she would surely give her life for her lord. The thought dispelled her care and made her happy. She was troubled only by the fear that her lord would not dare accept when she made the offer and that all three would refuse their permission when she told them.

She became so distraught at the possibility that her mother and father were awakened as on the previous night. They sat up, turned to her, and said, "See here, what is the matter with you? You are very foolish to become so distressed at a misfortune that can't be helped. Why don't you let us sleep?" They began to scold her thus, asking what good it did her to lament a situation that no one could put an end to or improve. With this they expected to silence the sweet maiden at once—they did not yet know her intention. "According to what my lord told us," she answered, "he can readily be saved. If you don't prevent me, I can be his remedy. I am a maiden and have this desire: I would rather die for him than see him perish."

The words saddened her parents. The father told his daughter to stop such talk since the deed was too much for her and she should make no promises to her lord that she could not keep. "You are a child," he declared, "and your loyalty in this is too great. You cannot carry out what you have said here. You have never known anything so loathsome. So be still. If you say anything more about it from now on, you will be whipped." He thought the command and the threat would make her be quiet, but they could not.

"Father," she replied, "as simple as I am, I have still enough sense to know from hearsay the painful truth that the death of the body is hard and bitter. But he who must endure hardships a long time is not fortunate either, for after he struggles along here and manages with great trouble to live to old age, he has to die just the same. If his soul is then lost, it would have been better for him not to have been born. I have a chance for which I shall always praise God: to exchange my young body for eternal life. You must nòt spoil it for me. I want to do myself and both of you a great deal of good by this. I alone can protect us from grief and harm, as I shall explain. We have the esteem and property that my lord's good will provides, for he has never said anything to hurt us or taken any of the farm. As long as he lives we shall be well-off, but if we let him die, we shall be ruined. I want to keep him for us by a wise action so that we all shall be saved. Now let me do this, for it must be."

When she saw that her daughter was in earnest, the mother said tearfully, "Dear child, remember the pain I suffered because of you and let me receive a better reward than that of which I hear you speaking. Temper your words or you will break my heart. You will forfeit all your bliss with God by that which you do to us. Think of His Commandment! He bade us love and honor mother and father and promised salvation for our souls and long life on earth as a reward. You say that you want to die to ensure our happiness, but you will wreck our lives, because you are the reason your father and I enjoy life. What good are life, property, and temporal joys to us if we do not have you? You must not bring us to grief, my dear daughter, but be our happiness, our carefree pleasure, a bright feast for our eyes, the delight of our lives, a flower among your kinfolk, and a staff of our old age. Should you willfully cause us to stand over your grave, you will be forever cut off from God's favor as punishment for your treatment of us. Daughter, if you want to be good to us, for God's sake give up the resolve I heard you declare."

"Mother," the maiden replied, "I trust you and father to show me all the kindness that a mother and father owe their child, and indeed I get this from you every day. Because of you, I have a soul and a beautiful body; indeed all who look at me praise me saying that I am the prettiest child they have seen in their lives. Whom, after God, should I thank for this but you two? So I will always gladly obey you. How great is my duty to do so! Mother, blessed woman, since I have you to thank for soul and body, let it be through your kindness that I remove them from the devil's power and give myself to God. This world's life is indeed the soul's ruin, but the worldly desire that leads to Hell has not yet touched me. I want to deliver myself up to God's power thus unstained and thank God for giving me in my youth the wisdom to hold this feeble life of little account.

"If I were to grow older, I fear that the charm of the world would drag me down to its feet as it has done to many others who have been betrayed by its sweetness. I would then perhaps become estranged from God. I lament to Him that I must live until morning, for the world pleases me little. Its comfort is great hardship, its greatest pleasure is heart-felt sorrow, its sweet reward is bitter distress, its long life is sudden death. We can be sure of nothing more than that today's well-being will be tomorrow's pain and that death always comes at last. That is wretched misery from which neither birth nor wealth nor beauty nor strength nor high spirits protect one: virtue and honor are no more defense against death than vice and low birth. Our life and youth are mist and dust, and our firm support trembles as a leaf. Whether man or woman, it is a depraved fool who likes to take in smoke, who cannot weigh this well and chases after the world. A fine, silk cloth has been spread for us here over the foul dunghill. Whoever is led astray by its splendor is destined for Hell and has lost nothing less than body and soul.

"Blessed woman, remember now your motherly faithfulness and allay the grief you feel because of me. Then father too will consider the matter. I know that he will grant me what is best, for he is wise enough to see that you will have me to enjoy for only a short time even if I remain alive. Should I stay two or three years with you before marrying, my lord will probably be dead and we shall perhaps be so distressed by poverty that you cannot give me enough dowry for a husband, except under conditions where I would live in such misery that you would rather that I had died.

"But let us not speak of the danger of something harming us and assume that my dear lord lives long enough for me to be given a husband who is prosperous and esteemed. Then you will have what you want and will think that I am fortunate, but my heart has told me something else. If I get to like him, it will be because I must and, if I dislike him it will be the death of me. It will thus be grievous for me in either case, and I shall be parted from a pleasant life by sorrow and by all those things that trouble women and keep them from being happy.

"So make the best arrangement for me, one that will never fail. I am courted by a free farmer to whom I would gladly give myself. Let him have me and my life will be well provided for: his plow tills well and his farm is fully equipped. Neither horse nor cow dies there, no crying children trouble one, it is not too hot or too cold, the aged become youthful and nobody gets older; it knows neither frost nor hunger nor any kind of sorrow—only complete and carefree joy. I want to go there and shun the farms that are beaten by thunderstorms and hail and washed by the floods with which one has always had to contend—where that for which one has worked all year can be quickly lost, in half a day. A curse on such husbandry! I want to leave it behind me.

"You love me, as is proper, and I would not like to see your love become my enemy. If you can see that I have the right idea and want me to enjoy wealth and honor, then let me go to our Lord Jesus Christ, whose mercy endures forever and who has as much love for poor me as for a queen. God willing, I shall never do anything to lose your favor. It is indeed His command, that I, having life from you, should obey you, and I shall gladly do so. But I also don't want to break faith with myself. I have always heard this said: he who makes another happy at his own expense and crowns another while degrading himself is much too loyal.

"However eager I am to do your will by being faithful to you, my chief duty is to myself. If you wish that which hinders my salvation, I would rather that you would weep a little because of me than that I should fail to show myself what I owe myself. I shall always want to go to that place where I find perfect bliss. You have other children; let them be your joy and console you for losing me, because no one can prevent me from saving my lord and myself. Mother, I heard you lament that your heart would be deeply distressed if you should have to stand over my grave. You will surely be spared this, for no one will let you see the place where I die. It will be in Salerno. My death there shall free the four of us from all danger. We shall be saved by death, and I far better than you."

When they saw that the child was eager to die, and when she spoke so wisely and contrary to nature, they began to think that no child's tongue could bring forth such views and such wisdom. They told each other that the source of her words was the Holy Spirit, who also cared for St. Nicholas as he lay in the cradle and taught him to turn his infant virtue to God. They thought in their hearts that her resolve had come from God and that they would not and should not hinder her from carrying it out. The farmer and his wife became cold with grief as they sat on their bed; love for their child so benumbed mind and tongue that for a time neither could speak a single word. The mother's sorrow caused her to be seized by cramps.

The two sat there, sad and distressed, until they saw that grieving would not help and that they might as well give their permission, since they could not change her mind. At least they could not lose her in a better cause. If they opposed her will, it could very easily harm them with their lord without having any other effect. They therefore readily declared that they were content with her purpose.

The innocent maiden was delighted. It was hardly daylight when she went to her lord's bedroom and called, "My lord, are you asleep?"

"No, little bride, but tell me, why are you up so early today?"

"Because of grief at your illness, sir."

"My bride," he said, "your treatment of me indeed shows that this troubles you—may God reward you—but there is no remedy for it."

"Truly, my dear lord, you shall have a very good remedy. Since your condition is such that one can help you, I won't let you wait a day longer. You told us, sir, that you could be cured if you had a maiden who was willing to die for you. God knows that I myself want to be the one: your life is worth more than mine."

The lord thanked her warmly for her good intentions, and his eyes secretly filled with tears of sorrow. "Little bride," he said, "death is not a light pain, as you perhaps think. You have convinced me that you would help if you could, and that is enough for me. I know your kind heart and that your purpose is honest and good, but I will not ask more of you. Although you cannot give me what you have promised, God will repay you for the loyalty you have shown me. Having tried so many remedies, I would be a laughingstock if this one were to fail me, as it surely would. Little bride, you are acting as children do: they are impatient and eager to attempt whatever comes into their heads, good or bad, only to regret it later. Yes, you too are like that. Your mind is filled with this plan now, but if one were to accept it and then want to carry it out, you probably would regret it."

He asked her to think it over a little more carefully and added, "Your father and mother cannot very well do without you, and I will not ask for anything that would grieve those who have always been kind to me. My dear bride, do what they advise you." He laughed as he said this, for he did not expect what was to come.

The noble man spoke thus to the maiden. However, her father and mother said, "Dear sir, since you have done us honor and been very kind to us, it would be a poor return if we did not repay you well. Our daughter is resolved to die for you and has persuaded us to let her do so. It is not a passing fancy, for this is the third day since she began urging us to give our permission. She has now won us over. May God cause you to be healed through her! We will give her up for your sake."

When it could be seen that his bride was serious in offering her life to cure the lord's sickness, there was much sorrow and display of grief. The child and the other three began to lament, but for different reasons. The father and mother wept long: the death of their beloved daughter was cause enough for them to weep. The lord too started to think earnestly of the child's loyalty and was overcome with such anguish that he wept bitterly and had grave doubts as to whether it would be better to carry out or give up the plan. The maiden also wept, for fear that he would be too faint-hearted to go on with it. Thus, all were sad and did not know what to do.

At last their lord, poor Heinrich, considered the offer and, to the maiden's great joy, accepted it. He thanked the three most sincerely for their faithfulness and kindness and prepared to set out for Salerno as soon as possible. All the things suitable for the maiden were quickly procured: beautiful horses and costly garments such as she had never worn before, made of ermine, samite, and the best sable to be found.

Who could fully describe the grief and mourning, the mother's bitter pain and the father's sorrow? It would indeed have been a distressing parting for them when they sent forth their dear, quite healthy child to die—never to see her again—if their misery had not been eased by God's perfect kindness, from which also came the child's resolve to go willingly to her death. It was not their doing, and, had God not taken all the sadness and pain from their hearts, it would have been a wonder that their hearts did not break. However, their sorrow became joy, and they suffered no more at the prospect of their child's death.

The maiden therefore journeyed happily with her lord to Salerno. What could trouble her now except that it was so far away and she had so long to live? When the lord had finally taken her to where the master was, as he had planned, he at once told him with joy that he had brought a maiden such as was required and let him see her. It seemed unbelievable to the master. "My child," he said to her, "did you come to this decision by yourself or were you driven to it by the command or threats of your lord?" The maiden answered that she had followed the counsel of her own heart.

Greatly surprised, he led her aside and charged her very strictly to say whether her lord had extorted the agreement. "My child," he said, "you must consider the matter more carefully. I'll tell you just why. If you should die unwillingly, your young life will be lost, and unfortunately it will not help us in the least. Now do not conceal your true will from me. I'll tell you what will happen to you. I shall take off your clothes, and you will naturally be very ashamed when you stand naked before me, then I shall bind your legs and arms. If you have any pity for yourself, then think of this anguish: I shall cut you open to the heart and tear it from your living body. Tell me, young lady, how you feel about that. No maiden ever endured such pain as you will suffer from me. I myself greatly dread what I shall do and see. Consider how it will be with you. Should you feel the slightest regret, my work and your death will be in vain." Again and again he warned her earnestly to give up her design if she was not sure she could hold out.

The maiden smiled because she firmly believed that death would this day help her escape from the troubles of the world. "May God reward you, dear sir," she said, "for telling me about the matter so carefully. In truth I am quite fearful and assailed by doubt. I'll tell you just what kind of misgiving has seized me: I am afraid that we shall have our trouble for nothing because you are faint-hearted. You are timid as a hare, your words are those of a woman, and your fear of seeing me die is much too great. Indeed, you are not doing justice to your great skill. Although a woman, I am strong: if you have the courage to cut me, I trust myself to endure it. I did not need you to tell me how fearful the torment would be, for I understood this well. Truly, I would not have come if I had not known myself to be resolute enough to bear it.

"Permit me to say that my weak nature has been taken from me and a spirit has come which is so strong that I stand here no more frightened than if I were going to a dance. For no torment to my body of a single day is so great that I would think that day too high a price to pay for eternal life up there. You will not be disturbed by anything I do; my resolve is too strong. If you believe you can restore my lord to health while giving me eternal life, for God's sake do it now. Let us see what a master you are. He in whose name it is to be done—I know well for whom I do this—strongly urges me on. He readily discerns service and does not let it go unrewarded. I know He himself says that whoever performs a great service shall have the greatest reward. I shall therefore consider this death to be a pleasant striving for so certain a recompense. I would be foolish to give up the crown of heaven, for I am of an humble family."

Since the master could now see that she was steadfast enough, he led her back to her sick lord and said to him, "Nothing can hinder us: your maiden is fully suitable. Be of good cheer, because I shall quickly heal you." He led her at once into his private quarters where her lord could not watch and locked and barred the door before him. He didn't want to let him see how she was to die. He bade the maiden undress in a chamber that was very well furnished with fine remedies. She was happy at this, tore off the ties of her clothing, and soon stood there naked but not the least abashed.

When the master looked at her, he thought to himself that there was no more beautiful creature in all the world than she, and he felt so sorry for her that his heart and mind almost lost courage. He then told the good maiden to climb upon a high table she saw standing there. The master bound her firmly to it and picked up a sharp knife, lying near, that he used for such matters. It was long and broad, but did not cut as well as he wanted. Since she was not to live, he was concerned about her pain and wanted to make death easy for her.

He had a fine whetstone at hand and began busily to sharpen the knife. Standing outside by the door, poor Heinrich heard the sound of the whetting, and it robbed him of all joy. He was deeply grieved that he should never again see the maiden alive. He searched until he found a crack in the wall and through it caught sight of her lovely body, naked and bound. He looked at her and at himself, and had a change of heart. What he had intended now seemed wrong, and his former spirit was quickly transformed into a new kindness.

When he saw that she was so beautiful, he said to himself, "You are foolish to want to live a single day against the will of Him whom no one can hinder. Since you must indeed die, you don't know what you are doing by not gladly enduring this odious life that God has ordained for you. Moreover, you also don't know whether the child's death will heal you. Let everything come that God has assigned you. I don't want to see the child die." He made up his mind about this at once and began to pound on the wall, demanding to be admitted.

"I don't have time now to open the door for you," was the answer.

"No, master, you must speak with me."

"I cannot, sir. Wait until this is finished."

"No, master, speak with me first."

"Just tell me what you want through the wall."

"Indeed, it can't be discussed that way."

He let him in at once. Poor Heinrich went to where he saw the maiden lying bound and said to the master, "This child is so lovely that I truly cannot see her die. May God's will be done with me. Let us allow her to stand up again. I'll give you the silver on which we agreed, but you must let the maiden live." The master of Salerno was glad to hear this and, obeying at once, untied her.

When she realized that she was not to die, the maiden's heart was troubled. In great sorrow she went beyond the bounds of decorum and manners as she beat her breast and tore her hair. Her conduct was so pitiable that no one could have seen her without weeping. "Oh! Oh, poor me!" she cried bitterly. "What will happen to me now? Must I thus lose the splendid heavenly crown that would have been my reward for this ordeal? Now I am dead indeed. Oh, mighty Christ, what glory has been taken from my lord and me! He and I are deprived of the honor that was intended for us. If this plan had been carried out, he would be cured and I would be forever happy."

So it was that she begged earnestly for death, but however urgently she desired it, her plea was in vain. When no one did her will, she began to scold. "I must pay for my lord's timidity," she said. "I have indeed seen how people have deceived me. Again and again I have heard them say that you were upright and kind and had a firm, manly spirit. So help me God, they lied. The world has always been mistaken in you, for all your life you have been an abject coward, and you still are. I can easily see this since I dare to suffer what you are not brave enough to permit. Sir, why were you alarmed when I was bound? After all, there was a thick wall between us. My lord, don't you trust yourself to endure another's death? I promise you that no one will harm you and that it will be useful and good for you."

However much she entreated and scolded, it could do her no good: she had to live. Poor Heinrich bore all the reproaches nobly, as a gallant knight who has never lacked good manners must do. When the unhappy stranger had clothed his maiden again and paid the doctor, as he had agreed, he set out at once for his own country. Although he well knew that he would find nothing but general disdain and scorn there at home, he left all that to God.

The good maiden had wept and lamented until she was near death when *cordis speculator,* to whom indeed no heart's gate is closed, perceived her faithfulness and her distress. Since He had chosen in kind wisdom to test them just as fully as the rich Job, our Holy Christ then showed how dear to Him faithfulness and compassion are by freeing both from all their sorrows and at once making the lord handsome and completely healthy. Through the care of our Lord God, the noble Sir Heinrich improved so much on the way that he entirely recovered and looked just like a young man of twenty. When they were thus made glad, he sent the news to those in his land whom he knew to be so gracious and kind that their hearts would be happy at his good fortune. They had cause to rejoice at the mercy God had shown him.

His best friends, who were aware of the lord's coming, walked and rode toward him for three full days so that they might receive him. They wouldn't believe anyone's report, only their own eyes, and they saw a miracle of God in the beauty of his body. If one wants to do them justice, one can well believe that the farmer and his wife did not remain at home. No one can describe their joy, for God had presented the two with a lovely sight, their daughter and their lord. There was never greater happiness than theirs when they saw that both were well. They didn't know how to act. Their greeting was strangely mixed with most unusual conduct, because their heart's delight was so great that tears rained down on their laughter. It cannot be denied that they kissed their daughter's lips somewhat more than three times.

The Swabians then received him with a praiseworthy gift, their cordial welcome. God knows that every honest man who has seen Swabians on their native soil must concede that there was never greater affection than that with which the lord's countrymen welcomed him on his return home. Why should I talk at length about what happened afterwards? He became much richer than before in both property and honor. He faithfully devoted all of his wealth to God and observed his precepts better than before. That is why his fame did not decrease.

The farmer and his wife also well deserved honor and wealth from their lord, and he was not so unjust that they did not get them in plenty. He at once gave them the broad farm, land and people, where he had stayed as a sick man. Justice required him moreover to provide his bride with goods, care, and all the things a noblewoman should have, or even more.

Experienced men then began to counsel the lord privately, recommending marriage. He replied that, if they agreed, he would send for his friends and conclude the matter in whatever manner they advised. He sent invitations and summonses in all directions to those who were subject to him and, when all were there—kinsmen and vassals—he told them what had been said. With one voice they stated that it was right and was time for him to marry. But then a great strife arose among those at the council, with one proposing this and another that, as people have always done when they are supposed to give advice. There was no agreement.

Sir Heinrich then said, "You all know well that a short time ago I was loathsome and offensive to people, but no one now avoids me, because our Lord's decree has given me a sound body. All of you must counsel me—for the sake of God, who has shown me His mercy by making me well—as to how I may pay my debt to Him."

"Resolve to make yourself and your wealth forever subject to Him," they answered. He had been looking very fondly at his dear bride, who was standing near, and now he embraced her and declared, "You have indeed all been told that I regained my health because of this good maiden whom you see here beside me. She is free-born, just as I am, and my whole heart advises me to marry her. God grant that this will please you. If so, I intend to have her as my wife. However, if it cannot be, I will die unmarried, for I owe honor and life to her. I ask by our Lord's grace that you consent." All replied with one accord that it was most fitting.

Enough priests were there, and they gave the maiden to Heinrich to be his wife. After a long and happy life, both went to dwell in the kingdom of Heaven. May this at the end be our lot. God help us to gain the reward they received.

Amen.

Moriz von Craûn

YOU HAVE OFTEN HEARD and have come to know with certainty this truth: that knighthood always was and always should be esteemed. We learn from books where it began and where it moved to later. The land in which the art of chivalry first appeared is called Greece, but it has since vanished from there. Knighthood sprang up in Greece when its armies besieged Troy because of a woman. One could indeed see there, so the story goes, many Greeks who constantly strove with like zeal for knightly fame.

Bold and stalwart warriors—Hector, Paris, Helenus, Deiphobus, and their brother Troilus—often defended the plain before their walls from the invaders and responded to the haughty Greeks in such a manner that the latter brought dead and wounded back to their camp. They struggled many years, for truly the attacks and defense of the Greeks never ceased. I would tell you still more about Troy, but what good would that do? We can let it go, because no one is able to relate it all. Even Dares—who was there, who wrote down and recited at night what had happened during the day, as he had seen it with his own eyes—could not tell the whole story of how the Trojans defended their land as long as Hector lived and protected them. However, when he perished, their renown faded greatly, day by day, for his heart was the heart of all.

Pandarus and Aeneas also contended fiercely for all to see, in the vanguard where heroic deeds were performed. Often there were so many fearless contests being fought before Troy that one could hardly see between the gleaming swords. That was no place for a coward, where warriors from many lands had to fight the defenders of the city constantly, for they struggled furiously then. Many faint-hearted men would have died without a wound because of their ceaseless fear. When the Trojans lost Hector, whom they had chosen as their protector, the position of the city worsened daily until it lay desolate. Wondrous things happened at Troy. That is a special story which I would be glad to tell in full if I could. Why haven't I done so? I don't know it well enough.

Knighthood can thrive only where it is loved, as was seen in Greece. It soon flees from the one who hates it, and did so from this land. When it tired of the decay there, it left. One must pay dearly when one gains honor through knightly deeds. That is a very old custom which, however, has lost nothing because of age, but renews itself daily, grows, and spreads afar. Honor and disgrace avoid one another. What the esteemed Alexander conquered for the Greeks, they gave up against their will, and their own worthlessness was to blame for their injury: they who once received tribute now pay it. A man should therefore hold fast to honor; it rewards without deceit.

Later there was no city in all the lands that could compare with Rome in power and splendor. It was famous. The proud Romans began to practice chivalry and realized at once that it afforded a noble enjoyment that became greater day by day. Knighthood abode in Rome after it was driven from Greece. As soon as it arrived there, Julius Caesar received it in knightly manner and conquered all the lands, so that they paid him tribute. His hand won greater praise than anyone else will ever gain as long as the world endures. Whoever is taught by his heart to do his very best gladly will surely succeed, but I see many men in this world living with no more honor than a beast. What good is life to such a man? He wastes both the happiness and the stores that God has given us all.

Rome's fame lasted until King Nero became ruler of the lands. He was a very wicked man who did everything, good or evil, that came into his head: nothing could prevent him from carrying out whatever his arrogance counseled. He had himself treated as a woman and indeed preferred men to women. Hear how he lay one day thinking about what it would be like for a woman to carry and give birth to a child. Since King Nero was most eager to know, he sent at once for his physician and asked, "How can you treat me so that I may have a child? You had better think of a way, for you will die if you don't."

"There is a very good medicine for that," the physician answered, "I shall fully carry out your order," and he gave him a powder that caused a toad to grow in his stomach. The king then started to bear a very heavy burden, although he might easily have been spared it, and when the toad commenced to grow large in him, he looked like a woman in front. Now he constantly regretted that he had ever begun this, for he feared the pains of labor. He therefore told the physician to abort the child and cure him. The physician did as he was ordered and helped the king to come out of it well and recover.

Nero was a tall man with large bones, and his mother was small. He thus always wondered where there could ever be a place in her so big that she could give birth to him. He had to find that out also and wouldn't rest until he ordered her cut open. She had to suffer this because of his wicked pleasure. He looked under the breasts and found countless wonders all the way down the body.

The king committed many outrages. Just hear what he did to destroy Rome. When he was told what had happened at the conquest of Troy, he sent for all his men and complained: "The Romans have wronged me so gravely that I indeed cannot rest until I see to it that they atone to me with their own ruin. Whoever helps avenge my grievance I promise to make very powerful and rich before I am through." Then his troops began a great battle against the lords of the city, as the king had commanded: he bade them set fires in many streets. He acted so unseemly because he wanted to see what had occurred at Troy. Rome was laid waste by the flames, and all the gallant men on both sides lay dead. Never in a thousand years had so much cruelty and shame appeared in their land as at that time: one still sees many deserted palaces. All Rome burned down because of a single man.

Knighthood then had to leave Rome, for it was poor in body and goods and had been robbed of its high spirits like an orphan by bitter hardships. It came to France in wretched state and lived there meagerly for a long time, until Charlemagne began to conquer the lands with his armies. Because of their bold courage, Oliver and Roland chose it as a comrade and practiced it in a knightly manner, for which they were highly praised. When their countrymen saw what fame the two had won, they followed their example, and thus all began to profit.

No one ever lived in a country which embraced joy more than France does, for their chivalry is noble. It is well-known and esteemed, and many other lands have greatly improved their knightly customs through its guidance. There they serve the ladies for pay in a most refined manner, because they are better rewarded in France than anywhere else.

Not long ago a knight lived there whose thoughts all turned to the love of a lady and whose heart counseled him to serve the countess of Beaumont at all times, for he found no one more highly regarded. This man, who is still famous, was named Moriz, and his ancestral home was at Craûn. He served her a long time eagerly and loyally, for tourneying and presenting gifts were his whole life, and he was always hoping to be rewarded. When he came into the borderland of France to take part in tournaments, there was no one on either side who did better or won more praise for it. He was handsome, well-mannered, courtly, prudent, and worldly-wise. He therefore behaved commendably, and everyone was rightly pleased with him.

Since things were going so well with him, he did as light-hearted gentlemen often do who love and gladly accept whatever they get in exchange. To be sure, the constant lover frequently wins both pain and distress. Still, if his faithfulness helps him to gain a reward that he has sincerely desired, then he is fully repaid for what he suffered before. That is now sweet and good, because he is richly compensated and is never pained by regret at having begun his suit.

Many people say with respect to this matter that all living things on earth, wild or tame, are destined to be subject to man and his wisdom. I thought so too before I learned that it can indeed not be. Without a blow Love forces a man to greater loyalty than an emperor could. So this man too was compelled to believe that he had to do and leave undone whatever Love commanded, whether it brought him comfort or distress.

Who is well acquainted with Love knows that she burns the heart in her fire: a man needs to be careful and consider how he can save himself from disgrace. Whatever harm befalls him, he must treat it as if it were nothing. You should know the truth of this, that one can never pay the price of honor by sparing one-self. Nobody now alive would expect to love without harm—he wouldn't have good sense, for Harm is the counselor of Love. If he is to carry out his affair to a happy ending, he who turns to Love should display much constancy until he persuades her to let him succeed with her.

I advise him who is in love and is wise to flee inconstancy and appeal to faithfulness. He will thus quickly take on a sweet burden, and all will end as he desires. There is much inconstancy in the world. I compare him who becomes fond of it to thieves: when one is hanged, the other does not consider limiting or giving up his stealing because of it. However often an unfaithful man sees a faithful one succeed, it means no more to him than a splash in the sea, for he wants nothing better.

I could warn you against much here, and must lament one thing more. Through the world a modish pair is moving that conquers many noble lovers, which is a wound to honor. Pray now that our Savior may turn them from the two! I'll tell you their names: Vanity and Error. May God keep them away from good people, who go to ruin because of them—I ask nothing for evil men, who will act according to their natures. Whoever becomes a companion of the pair because of inconstancy I call a faithless creature. They are not better together and become more wanton all the time: Vanity gives and Error takes. (No one could get me to do anything, even for pay, if it cost me some of my wealth.) A woman behaves the same way and soon creates want: who pays for shame with his property doubles the offense. Many people find fault with this price and rightly so, for it is a crime to forsake honor because of lust.

The nature of many men is such that, rather than suffer any kind of difficulty because of a good woman, they prefer to avoid them all. These men lack sense and think loss is profit. I would count it gain if, to further my happiness, I were to strive through service for honor or reward in courtly love. I claim this right for myself.

Sir Moriz knew how to maintain himself in a most courtly manner and therefore was sure to win honor from noblewomen, whose company he enjoyed: the reward of the vulgar is small. He chose one of them and served her a long time. Whoever serves and is able to profit by service, let him serve so as to benefit himself most and where one can reward him. Whatever rewards evil women give, they often make a man's soul and body joyless and of little worth. The good women give us high spirits and repay us with fame for whatever our service has cost. It is right that a courtly man who knows how to win their favor should serve them.

No matter what the faithful Sir Moriz had always earned from his lady, he still had to wait for his reward until he began to be uncertain and very unhappy. One night while lying alone and thinking about his trouble, he said, "I am sorry I was ever born. Am I to lose completely the hope I have always had? She whom I have served so much does not accept my efforts and is too late with her pay. I can therefore never be happy." Then he spoke again, "I am not prudent in this. From one land to another my service has brought me such praise that people have esteemed me as being noble, and my lady rewards me thus. What pay could be better! On the other hand I have to suffer some distress. How could I avoid it, for he who wants to strive for honor must give up ease. Still, if he wishes to escape sorrow, a man should consider carefully, and then everything will turn out well no matter how grievous his situation is. Taking thought is the best protection against trouble.

"It is quite clear that I am foolish and am wasting my time to no purpose. God knows that no one was ever so tormented as I, and I'll tell you how. I have always faithfully loved one who treats me as an enemy: as often as I implore her, I get only threats. How could I rejoice because of her, when I see myself in the distressing state where I can obtain neither a reward nor a promise from her for whom I have given up all other women? I serve and strive until it is the ruin of me. That is wretched grief. I would rather have a gentle death than to be chained like this. But it is she who must cure me; I must remain unrewarded by all women except her."

He thought thus about his lament: "What good does it do for me always to endure such terrible sorrow? I am the more foolish because of it. Whoever has become accustomed to care does not mind grieving, and that has happened to me. In this respect I must admit in truth that my heart has always been a coffer filled with sadness, that I have never lacked for pain, and that happiness has been a stranger to me. Indeed, my heart still knows nothing of joy except that I have often heard what has brought it to others. When I thought of it, I would gladly have done the same. This would make a Bavarian shilling out of each of my thousand sorrows. How could I endure them if my lady will not save me?

"It will be shameful if she will not tell me her intentions: I won't give her my life in exchange for death from longing. First, I'll see if she will allow me to be free of my trouble. Should her sweet comfort console me, then I would be forever proud and happy at last. However, considering what has happened up till now, I must be prepared for one thing (if I ever see the day I can speak to her): her heart may pay for my service with anger, for it is hard as flint. That is why fate has played vexing tricks on me with respect to her. But lack of faith robs me of comfort, and a most unwise resolve causes me to accuse a fate that still lies ahead of illtreatment. If fortune had been kinder, it would have spared me half of what I have suffered. Perhaps she will think better of it. Oh, if I could only know that before I see her!"

Filled with these misgivings, he came to where the lady stood. Listen to what happened as soon as he saw her: fear made him pale, then flush, then pale again. He changed color several times before he could say a single word, long or short, which annoyed the lady. "Why are you acting this way?" she demanded.

"Lady, I am unhappy."

"For what reason, or shouldn't you tell me?"

"No, lady, I just have to endure it."

"Speak. What is wrong with you?"

"Lady, do I have permission to say?"

"Yes. Tell me what troubles you."

"Lady, I am disconsolate."

"That can be very distressing for you."

"It is indeed, my lady."

"Is anything else the matter with you?"

"Yes, lady, I feel bad."

"Where?"

"All over."

"Then you should rub an ointment on yourself."

"I can't, for I know nothing of such things."

"But you are a strong man."

"Lady, my strength is gone."

"Would you like my advice?"

"Yes, lady, very much."

"Go to Salerno. There are many doctors in that place; if you are to recover, they will cure you. You may be sure of that."

"Lady, it is high time to stop this arguing, for I need a respite. I have lost my senses because of you, as you probably know, and you are now robbing me of my happiness. This is pillage that I am eager to avoid. Mistress of my joy, show me your kindness—which I greatly need—or I must die. I want you to reward me with death or with confident expectation; that is why I have come. Now I would like to hear how I am to leave, rich or very poor."

"Although I am not to blame for this," the lady replied, "I admit being indebted to you. All your life you have served me well and so much that I shall gladly pay you. You should know that I would do what might harm me forever, rather than remain the warden of your happiness any longer. For some time I have wanted to reward you as well as I can. A dependable man will become a thief for love of good pay. Because of your service, I must risk my honor from now on. It can't be helped, since 'thou art mine and I am thine.' Therefore do one thing for me," the countess continued, "and I shall never cease to repay you." He could hardly wait to learn what she wanted.

"Hold a tournament just outside the town," she said, "so that I can watch it here. Now arrange this soon, because I have never seen one. Be my knight here, and I'll reward you when I can." He then became a happy man. Without anyone noticing, she drew a fine ring with a precious stone from her finger and placed it on one of Sir Moriz's. The noblewoman wanted to indicate that she was marking him with it according to the customs of ladyloves. He took leave at once. She raised her beautiful arms, embraced him most tenderly, kissed him on the lips, and commended him to God's care. Her love put an end to his worry and distress and made up for all he had suffered because of her.

My lord Moriz von Craûn got himself many pages, who proclaimed this tournament in all the lands around. If I were able, I would now tell you just how the lord prepared for it. Using strange materials, he had a ship made that was to move over the fields without hindrance as if on the sea. This was done to excite wonder; the ship's master would have to have great wealth and knowledge to complete it.

Listen to how he devised the ship; I wish I could do it justice. Its keel was a wagon that held light beams, shaped in the form of a ship that might sail to Cologne. The master builder ordered these joined together and a deck laid. In it many holes were bored all around both sides where spears were to stand. So that the ship which was thus made could move, he constructed it as follows: a framework was built around it—on which it rested like a large building on a high foundation—so that one could drive it along on wheels.

The master had sent to Flanders for a fine, red fabric which made up all the outer walls. He went around and fastened it to the beams with good, long nails that were as white as silver: a ship needs many nails. He built this cloth ship with great care so that people would be pleased with it and ordered that the bow, the stern, and the high mast that was soon raised be solidly plated with gold. He attached a large rudder, as would be done with a real ship. He wanted to have still more gear for his vessel, as if it were to journey across the sea, so brass anchors and a railing of silk line were added. This was most unusual, and he could easily have dispensed with them as a vain waste, because the ship stood on a dry shore.

The people from far and near who saw this ship said, "What might that be? There is no Meuse or Rhine here: how will he send it on its way? Unless he is afraid of the Flood and wants to save himself in it, it is property lost. Of what other use could it be?" This news spread widely before the time of departure arrived.

When the ship was ready, it was decked out all over with the lord's coat of arms. All the helmsmen and seamen were dressed in his colors and looked as if their clothing had been made by the same tailor. I wish I could describe it to you rightly. He now ordered that the oars be carried on board and after them a wagon-load of spears. Three hundred of them, the color of the mast, had been kept separate from the others so that none would be lost. To each of these a costly pennon, like the sail, was tied at once. The lord ordered that they be placed upright in their holes and adjusted in the same way. The other spears were white. It was strange that he should want to use all of them up in one day in honor of the lady.

Without many people knowing it, he slyly brought into the ship the horses that were to pull it when they wanted to set out. Harnesses had been arranged between the cloth walls and the board floor, and the horses were hitched up there. That no one outside could see what was going on inside was a clever idea. The horses were so concealed that whosoever observed with his own eyes the ship moving would swear it was a dream. His shield was hung in the middle of the mast so that he would be recognized. The sail gleamed far across the land like a Lombard banner.

When the skipper came aboard, he directed the men to avoid completely the roads themselves, for easier passage, and to travel at all times over the open fields. The people then followed him, just as if it were a wedding celebration, and looked at everything there was to see. His sailors sang and rowed, but their labor went for nothing, because their strokes did not make the ship go any faster.

In this so knightly manner he journeyed through France to where the tournament was to be held. Many people gathered there—knights and ladies, old and young—to see the ship. A fair wind drove him to the field before the castle; he disembarked at once, and a tent was set up. His harbor was above a running spring by a meadow. It was not long until all the people came out of the castle with festive clamor and gazed at the skipper as at a strange beast.

His coat of arms was sewn to the cloth of the protective covering of his splendid tent. He would have been sorry to have left this behind because he could display it with honor. It was pitched on the grass with fine ropes. The knob was a mirror and the studs on the tent poles were of very hard sapphires. Beneath the tent lay long, broad quilts of splendidly ornamented sendal and gold on which the guests were to sit. Those who wished to enjoy his plenty were well received. A full cask of wine, as clear as could be, stood there, with a wooden cup floating in it so that everyone who was thirsty could get his own drink.

No other lord had ever treated the minstrels who came there so well: enough of these wanderers were in and before his tent to have carried off a house. When daylight was gone, so many large, wound candles were lit that they seemed to the people up in the castle a fire, as if a barn were burning. His tent gleamed in splendor. Had he been wearing the country's crown, it would not have been disgraced. Early in the morning the knights decided to come to the ship for mass. They did this, all together, which so pleased the skipper that he hardly knew what to do. A hen was roasted for each two knights. After they had eaten them and each had drunk his fill, the mass was sung and all hurried forth to arm themselves.

As soon as the lord of Craûn had the time and the room to do so, he put on a goathair doublet and asked for a soft felt cloth which he tied in front of his knees to protect them. He then had his legs enclosed in stockings of white mail. These were firm but not heavy, for he preferred light armor: he could spring about like a roe. He bound a fine girdle around his hips and fastened the stockings to it. They brought him a helmet which completely covered his forehead so that no one could even scratch the skin underneath. At last he drew on a hauberk, white as snow, and had the thongs tied very firmly with knots.

When all this was done, he boarded the ship with those whom he wanted to accompany him. A squire went to get his strong, handsome horse, brought it secretly to the door, and concealed it in the ship. The knight ordered that the others be led to a nearby hill where they were to wait for him. Then he had the sail turned toward the castle walls and set out with great pomp. They beat tambourines and sounded flutes and horns. No man was ever so angry but that this joyous music would have dispelled his ill humor. They blew long trumpets, and many notes rang out from pipes and rotes, as if the knight were leading a band of pirates and about to attack a ship on the sea.

Up in the castle, close to the gate, stood the countess's stately palace, which was beautifully adorned with marble. The windows were filled with ladies, in the midst of whom sat the one who had caused all this. "Do you know what is coming there?" she asked. "It is beautiful. I think that Saint Brandan has journeyed here to see miracles. However, let no one be dismayed if it is the Antichrist, because Judgment Day is near. Therefore do not listen to his words: we must have more faith in God."

The lord ordered that his craft be driven up to the mountain and near the palace. There he dropped anchor in order to hold fast to the land. When the knights learned that the ship had anchored, they rode onto the field. Why make a long story of it? There was such a crowd around the ship that they hardly had room to contend. The tournament had attracted many knights, who were evenly divided between the two sides. As soon as it began, the count came down from the castle and, while his wife was looking on, happened to kill an opponent with his spear. This made them both very sad. The count clearly showed his grief, weeping bitterly that he should ever become laden with guilt because of knighthood, and took off his armor at once. He rode to the castle, disheartened at his sin.

Everyone was unhappy at the distressing event, but the skipper who had sailed there over land urged them to continue. "My ship and I have come to be present," he said. "See what an honor that is for you. You would never live down the shame if I were to drown on dry land." Then one after another said that it would be most unusual if the tournament should be ruined. "What if a man has died? Let us commit his soul to Saint Michael and joust." All advised as he had desired.

A great clamor arose from the lists as many helmets and shields resounded and many men were unhorsed. When the lord in the ship saw a host of bold knights wielding swords and spears out on the field, he put on a surcoat of fine samite that shown brightly. It was wide, well-cut, and displayed a skillfully wrought coat of arms that had the most elegant border you have ever heard of.

He tied on a helmet that suited him well. It was artfully decorated and embellished with so much gold that one could see it gleaming from afar. Anybody would think from his appearance that it was a king sitting there. They brought the knight a horse that was white as a swan and that wore a coat of sendal—he had eight others outside with equally fine trappings. He then ordered his men to bring the ship quickly to the thick of the conflict. Forward in the bow of the ship a door had been cut from which the knight now rode alone and in splendor. His company had been small when he sailed across the land, but later it had become much larger. Some of his squires came running up with one or two spears in their hands as a real battle began. He hurriedly seized his shield and a colored spear, spurred his horse forward in a fearful rage, and fell on the enemy just like an eagle on a flock of small birds.

The knight struck down one man, another, and then the third and fourth together. He unhorsed the fifth with great force, the sixth with even more, and went on to strike down the seventh and eighth. He knocked the ninth far from his horse in the midst of his friends and the tenth onto the grass. Everything fell before him. He fought with such success that all around him there were horses running riderless like a herd of breeding stock. As soon as his steed began to sweat, he gave it away and mounted another; and when he moved on to the next horse, somebody appeared at once to accept the one he had left. The skipper thereby earned the noisy support of all the wandering minstrels, through his gifts as well as his prowess.

After using up all his colored spears in regular jousts—as the lady had requested when she kissed him—the knight started on the white ones. She indeed owed him thanks, for no man ever won such great praise as he received then from both sides. Even if he had been a real heathen, outside of Christianity, whoever saw him that day would have granted him the honors, and rightly so. While he was flying around like a ball, he had the heralds announce everywhere that those who wanted gifts should go to the ship. Throughout the day they were given there whatever they desired of the things he had brought.

When evening approached, the knight retired to his tent to rest, because he was weary from wielding sword and spear. Since he knew how to satisfy with his wealth and good will anyone who asked him for a present, he was praised everywhere. He told the pages to take the ship in which he had ridden there, saying, "Who could deserve it more than you?" But as soon as they laid hands on it, a host of wanderers also hurried up. So many that no one could count them. The first got two yards of cloth, the second and third three, and the fourth enough for a coat. The fifth broke the head of the sixth, the seventh seized the mast, and the eighth the rudder. The ninth obtained the cloth for a vest, and the tenth only enough to make an ornamental hem. With such honors it was divided among them. You never before heard of so famous a ship that was never in the water.

Some time after the tournament was over, a man who had been taken captive came and begged for something from the knight. The latter pulled off his hauberk, gave it to him as a present, and received his heartfelt thanks. On removing the hauberk, he quickly drew his surcoat over his shoulders because of the cold. He waited to see if somebody would appear to take his stockings too, but no one came. He then untied the thongs on one leg. Those who had accompanied him had left him entirely alone since they had heard him say that they were to give whatever they had to whoever asked for it. For this reason no attendants were there to care for him.

While he was taking off the stocking, a messenger arrived and, finding him alone, said, "My lady has sent for you. Come now, the time is here. She told me to tell you to come to her just as you are." The knight was most happy to do this: he mounted the squire's horse and rode forth as he had been ordered. Now listen to where the squire left him—in an orchard. Waiting here at the lady's command was a pretty maiden who asked him to go with her to a room which the two women had secretly chosen for the assignation. The maiden led the hero there. On every side the walls were so covered with fine murals that the place had the splendor of a cathedral, and the ceiling was decorated with mosaics until it was as bright as a mirror inside both night and day: as if the ceiling had windows of precious stones.

The two went in alone. A bed was standing in the middle of the room; hear how it was made. The posts were large, round, and inlaid with the raised, ivory figures of every kind of beast on earth. They were framed by the gold in which the ivory had been mounted. The crosspieces were of a wood Vulcan cannot burn, and over them were stretched four leopard skins—that only very rich people have—held together by seams. All this is true, although I can't prove it. On the skins lay much large, soft bedding which was covered with elegant silk from Greece. On top of it was a quilt—I don't think Lady Cassandra or any of her race ever made a better—and a bedspread of fine, white linen. this had a border of coal-black sable a span wide above and a down fur below that was splendid and costly. The beast from which the pelts came is called an alfurt and is caught only in a land named Carthage, far across the sea, that was once ruled by Lady Dido and now belongs to the king of Morocco. Where the heads lay, the bed was made higher with a silk bolster.

The bed could well be finer than I have described, but I can do no better than to leave it as it is. In splendor it was like the one that Heinrich von Veldeke made so well for King Solomon, on which he was lying asleep when Lady Venus called and awakened him. She startled him out of his sleep with her bow when she shot him in the heart, causing pain that distressed him the rest of his life. However wise he might have been, he had to submit to her fetters because she robbed him of his senses. It was very little better with this man, who was sitting beside the maiden under such intimate and strange conditions.

Grass, leaves, and rushes were strewn on the flagstones. The two entertained each other with conversation, speaking in turn. At times she would ask him questions, and then he would inquire about all sorts of things. "This is certainly a splendid palace," the knight said, "lovely and delightful. It truly seems to me that it would be just what I would ask for, could I get my wish: that my lady were here. But I would think any house on earth, however humble, to be better than this if I once saw her go into it."

"As bad as things are with her husband," replied the maiden, "she will come as soon as she can. My lord has been in bed all day, weeping bitterly. He doesn't think he will ever be happy again since, because of you, he had the great misfortune to kill a knight. He therefore sorely laments the fact that your journey was ever undertaken and constantly curses the building of the ship. So it is that my lady must be very careful if you two are to carry out your agreement in all respects."

"My journey didn't harm your lord," said the knight, "nor has it helped me yet. But I know one thing indeed: as far as I can judge, he is a man of courtly manners who, if he were told of all I have done for his wife and knew that I were here, would command her to go to me, however much he might miss her and even though he had killed nine men." The knight sat there—sad and weary, angry and sullen—and made a motion as if he were about to lie down and be comfortable for a while. Seeing that he was annoyed, the maiden said kindly, "Why don't you lay your head in my lap and rest until my lady comes? Since you are tired and weak, it will perhaps do you good."

"I would do it if I could be sure of awakening before my lady came and found me asleep. If my nap were to cost me her favor, I would never be happy again."

"Leave it to me," answered the maiden. "I'll take care of it."

"Will you?"

"Yes."

"Then I'll go to sleep." Since she had given her permission, he then laid his head in her lap and at once fell asleep. His trouble was that he had spent so many long nights thinking about how to carry out his wasteful project with the ship and how to gain honor from that to which he had devoted a great deal of thought.

He had not lain there long when the noblewoman, who could easily have come sooner, arrived in secrecy and fear. The maiden started to awaken the weary man as soon as she heard her lady's steps, but the latter saw her and, hurrying up, ordered her not to disturb him. Then they discussed the tired knight. "I know it is true," said the beautiful lady, "that no one ever served a woman better than this man has served me: if I were to leave him unrewarded, it would be a sin for which I could never atone. I therefore heeded his lament to the extent that I was going to pay him today for his labors. Here I am, ready to do so, and he lies there like a dead sheep. He prefers sleep to me. If he had been able to do without it, I could have depended on him: I have learned that. As it is, I am not going to take the risk. If I had been so dear to him as he claimed, he would have waited better for me. No rest will cost him as much this year: whatever good it may do him later, his sleep has taken me away from him."

"I lament this before God, dear knight," spoke the maiden, "for my lady has given a hard sentence. You went to sleep trusting in me! How can I ever make up for my failure? I shall always deeply regret that you, tired and battle-scarred, were

placed in my care, since you are to lose the reward for all your service because of
me. Oh that I was ever fated to harm you so! Believe me, lady, should people learn
of this shameful deed, you will never regain your honor: you may be sorry if you
behave in such an uncourtly manner. I don't believe any man alive will serve any
more for a lover's pay when he hears about this. Your anger is not well directed.

"It is displeasing to us women that this evil should burden the world because of
you: that men will rely on none of us any longer. Now see how that would become
you. You shouldn't make him suffer for it. It is in the nature of men that they do
less for women than suits us. For God's sake, lady, consider well: there is no one
here but us three. Bid him get up. If he has lost, then perhaps sixty more have
lost, knights who would gladly endure hardships for noblewomen if they were to
get a reward. Should they be robbed of it because of you, it is most unfortunate
that you came when you did. What is the world without the wages women give?
Were King Solomon living, he could not offer better advice than mine: if the
knight is asleep, what of it?"

"I am sorry I ever became so much involved with courtly love," replied the
countess. "I am afraid it will bring me harm. This is quite likely to follow the one
who is too eager to pursue courtly love. I'll tell you what happens to those who give
way to sexual passion: they make themselves prisoners, just like the man who
spreads a net and falls into it himself. I intend to guard against that. I would
rather be free than belong to a man, for men are disloyal. Whatever I were to do
for this knight would amount to a public confession. Tomorrow probably three
or four people would learn of our 'wedding' and very soon after thirty more: my
honor would thus be sacrificed for nothing. Therefore I'll remain just as I am."

"You have spoken of the worst thing that can happen to you later," the maiden
replied, "when you should expect the best: it would be proper for him to avoid
them all. We, however, must still observe the old custom and do as women have
always done. Now wake him, for it is getting late. Even though you are still
unconquered, you know that in the end Love is the master of all reason."

"I am not afraid of her power and do not believe she will ever overcome me
either by entreaty or by force. So see to it that the man lies here until I am gone,
after that tell him to get up and go home. Bid him be more careful: it will profit
him in the future." With this she departed. The good maiden was sad that the
esteemed lord had not benefited from his devotion and fearful because he was to
leave, unrewarded and forsaken, after having asked her to watch for him.

Just then the knight awakened from a dream and, as soon as he looked up, said
to her, "I never had such an oppressive sleep. I fancied that my lady was here and
would not speak to me. How could I ever get over that? If I were to lose her favor
now through my own fault, I would grieve the rest of my life."

"Oh!" cried the maiden. "One tired and the other unfit, we both have failed. My
lady has behaved poorly and may have harmed herself forever because of it: a
woman's anger has cost her her honor. But I indeed hope that she has since

regretted her command. She came on me very quickly and without warning. Truly, I was afraid she would be offended and was looking all around, but she slipped up on me just like an incubus. She was pale with fear, but it may have been wrath that made her vacillate."

"You should have wakened me."

"I would gladly have done so if she had not strictly forbidden it. I was frightened almost to death."

"Why couldn't she have acted kindly! Now for the first time I clearly see her disloyalty. My service has been in vain," said the highly praised knight, "and I must always endure the burden of the injury done me. But what did she tell you to say to me?"

"She said only that I should let you lie for a moment and then bid you go back to your quarters."

"It would be strange indeed if I were to get any rest now that this has happened to me. Because of sleep, my misfortune will truly be awake for a long time. Lady, since you are at fault, do just one thing for me."

"Lord, I shall do it if it can possibly be done."

"My lady has made me unhappy, believe me. In the name of God go back to her and beg her for the sake of every woman's honor to restrain her anger and not leave me like this. It will be a painful story if she won't have pity on poor me. The pay she has given me too rashly for my error is more than I can bear." He urged her with pretty entreaties until she did it for him.

With tears flowing onto her hands and sleeves, the maiden sadly returned to her lady. However, although she bitterly lamented the latter's shameful deed, she acted prudently, as the knight had asked her to do: she tiptoed very quietly up to the bed in which the lady lay, lifted the covers, and gently touched her hand. As soon as the lady felt the touch, she said, "Where did you come from and what do you want now?"

"Lady, I am his messenger and want to beg you in the name of the God who gave you soul and body to honor all women and not let him lose his suit thus. You can calm the anger of the three of us by going to him, as becomes you. However hard a heart might be—though it be as unyielding as a diamond—it would become soft if it saw the grievous harm you have done him and heard his laments."

"Now believe what I tell you: his injury can easily worsen. Should my lord wake up and find him here, the knight will never leave alive. So if he is wise, let him go back as he came. You don't know what you are chattering about and are making a fool of yourself. Now be still, for I am going to stay here and sleep until morning." Vexed, she turned over and acted as if she were sleeping. The maiden sighed deeply and silently walked away, weeping because of this affront.

Annoyed at the delay, the knight had followed her to the door and was waiting there for her. When he heard her story, his heart was deeply troubled, but he spoke out as an upright man: "Lady, I commend myself to God, for life means nothing to me. I'll speak with her myself or leave it here. I shall go in there to her and find out how I have done wrong." He pushed the door open with a hard shove and quickly entered the bedroom. This night, as always, a candle was burning there in a glass.

The knight did not make a splendid appearance, as I shall explain. He had been so hard pressed by blows that the blood had run from his forehead down over his eyes, with much collecting on his brows. In his wrath the esteemed nobleman looked like a lion creeping up on his prey when he moved stealthily toward the two sleepers. Greatly distressed, the count had lain there as a troubled man who cannot sleep for grief. He had struggled so with his thoughts that he had often started up and looked around in terror. Afterwards, he slept fitfully but not for long.

As Sir Moriz came closer to the lady—in a bloody surcoat that had been slashed and stabbed almost to pieces—one of his mail stockings, the one on the right leg, rang out against the stone floor. The count looked up and cried out, too frightened to utter an incantation. He woke his wife with his clamor: "Wherever he came from, the devil is here with us, or the raging host. If God doesn't save us, we shall die." He was more afraid than his wife, who knew the hero at once. "Who goes there?" cried the count.

"I'll be glad to tell you: I am the one you killed. You must be my companion in hell forever. Since you dispatched me thither, it cannot be helped." When this apparition appeared to him, the lord of the castle sprang up from his bed in great alarm and bumped his shin so hard that he lay in a faint the rest of the night. Seeing what had happened, the knight went to the bed and said, "This is half empty. I don't know who should be here, but it is where I shall rest." Then he drew back the covers and slipped in with the lady. She was greatly surprised and, moreover, in this distressing situation did not know whether her husband were alive or dead. She dared not go to him, for the bold knight had robbed her of her wits, but she did answer.

"You are the most daring man I ever heard of," she said, "to attempt such a risky venture. You didn't ask if I wanted you to do this or not. It seems to me so strange that people will be talking about it until Judgment Day." However she was thinking, "Since things have turned out this way, it can't be helped: I'll have to let him do his will with me. Well, I'll submit in a friendly manner and dispel his anger." She kissed him once and then again. Then she spoke to him, but when he did not reply to any of her questions she tired of this and put her arms around him. The knight too began to warm up now and he did something with the lady: I don't know what. At any rate, why should I tell you? You are quite aware of what goes on under such conditions, and it might as well be left unsaid.

Afterwards the bold warrior stood up and quickly took from his white hand a ring the lady had given him. "Take back your gold," he said, "for I shall not be your lover. You are ruthless. Until now I have always been devoted to you and have gladly done everything I could to serve you. If all were like you, I would never serve a woman again. Now go to your ailing husband and live without honor. I won't punish you anew for having robbed me so shamefully of my reward." The knight thus took his leave. Later he travelled about even more than before, when he was trying to gain the lady's favor, and won praise and honor with all sorts of extravagance.

Since people spoke highly of him, she began to regret having caused him pain. Indeed, she felt such remorse that everyone noticed the change in her color. "It is only just that I should suffer," she thought, "and have sorrow instead of great love. I brought this grief on myself. If I should once again wish for a man to serve me, how could he be more suitable for a woman or more highly born than the one I have lost? I therefore curse the day when my unjust quarrel harried me until it conquered me. I have brought shame on myself that I would gladly do without. However, I shall endure the disgrace as long as I live unless God grants me such wisdom and good fortune that the knight will really love me. The maiden could see this and acted in all loyalty. How one honors oneself who gives aid to a friend for whom things are going badly! And help in time is better than that given after the man has perished."

This was at the beginning of summer. The birds in the forest sang clearly and boldly with many voices, and the roses and heather outdid each other in blooming. It was just the season when one cannot endure sorrow. The forest had again decked itself out to greet the summer in beautiful attire. Green foliage, grass resplendent with a mass of all kinds of blossoms, the sweet song of the birds: these fill with cheer everyone who is looking forward to happiness.

Early one morning when she could not sleep for care and remorse, the lady got up and, driven by her sorrow, went alone to a gallery that hung over the castle wall. She stood there at a window, as pining women often do who, like her, have endured sorrow because of love: one can see them grieving. She laid her cheek in her lovely white hand and listened to the beautiful song of the nightingale. "Happy is he who is destined to live joyfully," she said, "as I would be doing if I had allowed myself to. However, now I must waste my entire youth with great loss of honor. Whom do I have to blame that from now on I must be subject to a tiresome life and serve it to no purpose? The one who caused it: myself, and I can only cry out to God in sorrow."

Meanwhile the maiden, who also had gone out for a walk, quietly approached and heard the lady's lament. However much at fault her mistress might be, the maiden nevertheless was so troubled by her grief that she could not remain there, but wanted to go back in: her complaint was too pitiful. Just then the lady looked around and quickly spoke: "Have you been here long?"

"Yes. I heard all that was in your heart, and it distresses me. What I told you was true. You couldn't believe it, but remember how I advised you."

"I do, and I know in truth that the only one who could make me joyful now is He who blots out my sin just as He quiets the waves of the sea. I shall always be sad unless it should happen that He destines me for happiness and in kindness appeases the man for whom I grieve day and night. I am sorry I ever caused him pain, but my remorse comes too late. I should have taken your advice. He who acts on his own, according to his own desires, and without seeking counsel, will regret it just as I do. I used to think that the cause of women should rightly prevail, and that is why I have come to grief. However, I have not done what is right, and he has avenged himself by leaving me. My heart will be filled with sorrow and distress as long as I live. It was my fault that I fell into this snare. I therefore advise all of you who may undertake a love affair in the future to consider my sorrow and take care not to suffer the same fate."

Well let us bring this story to an end. The German language is not rich, and whoever wants to compose in it must tend to his rhymes, splitting some words apart and putting others together. I would do this more skillfully if I could.

Heinrich von Kempten

THERE WAS ONCE AN EMPEROR named Otto who was so powerful that many lands paid him fearful homage. His beard was long and beautiful, for he took very good care of it, and whatever oath he swore by it he always kept. He had red hair and was in all respects an ill-natured man. He had a quick temper, which he often showed; he who opposed him in anything was sure to lose his life. When the emperor cried at someone: "By my beard, you shall pay for it!" that person died at once, because he would then receive no mercy. The emperor had thus taken the lives of many who had lost his favor through a serious offense.

Once at Easter time he arranged a festival in his large and stately castle of Bamberg. A host of worthy abbots therefore left their monasteries to come to the emperor's court, and many esteemed bishops hurried there with great pomp. Also a splendid troop of counts, barons, and servant nobility—all subjects of the empire and its lord—arrived in a joyous throng. By the time the priests had finished singing the Easter mass all the tables were festively prepared. Bread and many fine cups had been placed on them so that Emperor Otto could wash his hands and eat just as soon as he came out of the cathedral with his crowd of princes.

A young noble had been sent to Bamberg to learn courtly manners. He was good-looking and honorable, and everyone there gave him high praise that was without guile. He was the sole heir of the many estates of his father, the mighty duke of Swabia. On this day the handsome boy went along the tables at the court and touched them with his fair hands. He then picked up a loaf of white bread and broke off a small piece to eat, just as all children do, who want to nibble on something beforehand. The lord high steward of the emperor was going by, distributing what was to be eaten when the mass was over, and noticed that the duke's son had taken the bread. He at once became very angry, for it was his habit to let any little thing upset him. He ran at the beautiful boy and struck him so hard on the head with the staff he carried that the crown of his head and his hair became wet with blood. He fell down and sat there weeping bitter tears because the steward had dared to strike him.

This was seen by an excellent knight named Heinrich von Kempten, who had a noble and very manly spirit. He had come with the boy from Swabia, so I have read, for he was his tutor and was teaching him to be worthy of the greatest respect. Filled with sorrow and rage that his highborn ward should be beaten so mercilessly, the bold knight spoke angrily to the steward: "What did he do that you should disgrace courtly manners by striking the son of a noble prince with such brutality? I'll tell you flatly that you are not acting as you should when you strike my lord for no reason."

"That doesn't concern you," answered the lord high steward. "It is certainly my duty to control ill-bred rogues and thrash anyone who behaves badly here at the court. You can stop such talk at once: I fear you just as little as a hawk does a chicken. What will you do about my striking the duke anyhow?"

"You'll find out soon enough," said Heinrich von Kempten. "You are going to be sorry right now that you dared to beat the noble prince, for I won't put up with this any longer. You wicked scoundrel, how can you presume to live after having given the boy such fierce blows? Since your uncouth hand has acted with such vulgarity, your blood will flow over this spot and the entire hall." He then seized a stick, a large cudgel, and struck the steward so hard that his head was crushed like an egg and his skull split in two like a piece of pottery. He whirled around and around as a top does--I imagine that his head and brain were completely shattered—then fell on the stone floor and lay there a miserable corpse as the hall became red with his blood. This caused a great uproar.

In the meantime the emperor too had come, washed his hands, and sat down at the table. When he saw the fresh blood on the floor, he asked, "What happened here? Who befouled the hall and made it so bloody?" His chief servants at once told him that the lord high steward had just been slain. The emperor then said angrily, "Who caused me this distress?"

"It was Heinrich von Kempten," they all cried.

"Well," said the mighty emperor, "if he killed my steward, then he has come to us a bit too early from Swabia. Have him brought before me at once. I want to ask him why he has done me this great injury."

The knight was therefore summoned to appear before the dreadful emperor. As soon as Otto saw him, he burst out fiercely: "Sir, what madness is this, that you should murder my exalted lord high steward? You have incurred my great disfavor and shall feel the severity of my imperial might. You have damaged my renown and the esteem of my court. You will be punished for this outrageous deed, the killing of the steward."

"No, my lord," replied Heinrich von Kempten undaunted. "Let me gain here your pardon and lasting goodwill. Be so kind as to hear me before judging me guilty. If I have deserved your enmity through undue violence, then your great power can destroy me. However, if I can prove that I am not to blame, deign to be gracious and do me no evil. For the sake of Him who arose on Easter, permit me to try to win your imperial favor. Since you are so wise as to be naturally prudent, honor this festival and the worthy nobles here by showing mercy to me today in my misfortune. No offense was ever so odious that it could not be forgiven; let me therefore find deliverance here so that I need not die."

The evil, red-headed emperor answered him from a heart filled with wrath: "The death-pangs my steward suffered here cause me such distress that I have no desire to forgive your crime. My imperial favor will forever be denied you. By my beard, you will atone for having needlessly killed him."

The noble Heinrich fully understood by the emperor's oath that he was indeed about to die, and this made him very angry. Since he knew that the monarch kept every vow made by his beard, he decided to do all he could to defend himself and save his life. "Now that I know that I have been condemned to death," he said, "it is time for me to protect myself while I can." With this the excellent knight quickly sprang at the emperor, seized him by his long beard, and jerked him across the table. Whatever had been placed before the emperor was thrown to the dirt as he was dragged by the beard. His chin and lips lost a great deal of hair, and his imperial head was sorely abased; the splendid crown it had worn fell to the floor along with all his rich finery. Heinrich at once dropped on top of him, drew a sharp knife, and swiftly put it at the emperor's throat. He began to choke him with the other hand.

"Now promise me your pardon and good will," said the knight, "or you will die right here on the floor. Take back the oath you just swore, if you want to live. Otherwise this will be the end of you." He held the emperor down and pulled mightily on his beard, choking him so much that he couldn't speak. The brave and noble princes all sprang up and ran to where the emperor lay, pale as death, beneath Heinrich. They wanted to free the exhausted man from him at once.

At this the knight declared: "If anyone touches me, the emperor dies, and then I'll tend to him who first attacks me. Since I am to lose my life, your lord shall perish. This good knife will separate him from the imperial crown. Those of his guests who try to kill me will also pay, for I'll spill rivers of their blood before I'm finished. Come on! Let him who wants to die just come and touch me!" They all retreated then, as necessity demanded; the emperor too, with great effort, motioned frantically for them to step back.

When the nobles had done this, the undaunted Heinrich again spoke to the emperor: "Should you want to go on living, don't have me lie here any longer. I'll spare your life in exchange for assurance that I shall be safe. If you don't give the surety, it will be your death." At this the emperor at once raised his hand and swore on his imperial honor that he would let the knight depart unharmed and without delay.

As soon as the oath was taken, the knight released the imperial beard and let Otto get up from the floor. The latter then went to sit down again on his splendid throne and, smoothing his hair and beard, spoke thus to the lord from Kempten: "I have promised to let you go without harming you. But take care that your path never crosses mine and that I never catch sight of you again. I can easily tell that you are too burdensome to be a part of my retinue. Indeed, your treatment of me was quite unseemly. Anyone who looks at my beard will readily see that I would always be happy to forgo a close association with you. You will never be my barber, believe me; and your razor will never trim my beard again, by God. It cuts so roughly that it tears away both hide and hair, even of kings. I have learned very well that you are a poor barber. You must leave my court and this land at once." The knight therefore said goodbye to the emperor's retinue without delay and hurried off.

He returned to Swabia to settle down on a prosperous fief. He had fields and meadows at Kempten, so I have read, and was a vassal of the monastery there. A reliable text reports that he lived very well, for he had enough income and was highly respected.

Ten years later, as luck would have it, Emperor Otto was carrying on a great war and laying siege to a splendid city beyond the mountains. He and his army vigorously attacked the fortress with catapults and arrows for a long time; at last, however, he became so short of men that he began to send out for more German knights. He ordered it announced to the nobles everywhere that all who then held lands in fee from the empire should come quickly to his aid. He also informed the princes that those who had received fiefs from him and owed him military service were to hurry at once to Apulia and help him in the battle there. Whoever did not do so would lose his fief. While this message was being proclaimed in all German lands, a herald was sent to bring it to the abbot of Kempten.

When the worthy lord heard the emperor's order, he made preparations for the expedition and also (according to the report) quickly called upon all his vassals to keep their oath of fealty by accompanying him. He summoned the wise Heinrich and said, "You surely have heard that the emperor has sent to the German lands for troops and that I am one of the rulers who are to journey over the mountains to help him. For this I need you and your vassals. I therefore now direct them, and you first of all, to join this expedition that I—and you—have been ordered to undertake. So you must get ready to travel at once."

"Oh, my lord, what have you said!" cried the knight. "You know very well that I dare not appear at the emperor's court, for I am greatly out of favor with him. For the sake of the services I have already rendered you must excuse me. The emperor has completely withdrawn his favor from me and spread over me the cover of his displeasure. I have raised two sons whom I shall send with you: you will take two men there, both splendidly equipped for battle, in the place of one."

"No," replied the abbot. "I am not disposed to accept them instead of you, because you will be of more use to me. You are the one on whom I must rely at this time to preserve my esteem. You give very good counsel in battle and can arrange the important matters that one has to take care of at court better in every respect than anyone else. I need no one for this journey as much as you. I therefore ask that you help me with wise counsel. If you object and refuse me your service, God knows I'll give the fief you have from me to someone who is not afraid to earn it."

"Truly," said the knight then, "if it is a matter of obeying you or losing my fief to someone else, I would rather go with you, however great the danger to which the expedition may expose me at this time. Sooner than give up property and position, I'll ride with you even to death. You shall have the help in need that my duty requires me to render, for you are my lord and I must serve you. Since you insist, your wishes will be carried out. In order that I may faithfully serve you in the campaign, I'll gladly bear whatever evil the emperor may do to me." At this the brave man equipped himself for the journey and rode away over the mountains with his lord. The knight was so bold that he left nothing undone because of fear: he followed the abbot's orders and was subject to him in every way.

Soon they reached the city that the emperor was besieging with his mighty army. Once there, Heinrich always avoided the emperor, for his offense and the resulting enmity caused him to be afraid of the monarch and stay out of his sight. The brave knight therefore had his tent pitched at a little distance from the rest of the army.

One day, so I have read, a bath was prepared for him, because he needed some comforts after his journey. While the knight was sitting in the tub, which had been brought to him from a village, he saw the great emperor ride swiftly toward some people who were coming out of the city: he wanted to talk with them and parley about the city. However the treacherous citizens, with guile and cunning, had plotted his death and were ready to murder him without warning as soon as he began to speak with them. It was only a moment, I assure you, before he rode up quite unarmed. A hidden danger lay in wait for him there, and he came upon the ambush suspecting nothing. He was shamelessly attacked: the faithless people who had secretly planned his death rushed at him with bare swords to do him harm.

When the knight of Kempten saw that they had treachery and murder in mind and, in a breach of faith, were going to kill Emperor Otto, he left off bathing, sprang out of the deep tub (like the excellent warrior that he was), ran quickly for the shield that hung on the wall, and seized his fine sword. With these the naked knight dashed to the aid of the emperor. Although quite nude, he freed and defended his lord, cutting down many of the people who had tried to kill him. With valiant hand he caused many streams of blood to flow as his mighty blows drove some to their death and put to flight all who remained alive. As soon as the knight had rescued the emperor, he ran naked back to the tub, sat down in it as if he knew nothing in the world about the incident, and went on bathing as before.

Meanwhile the emperor fled to the army: he had not recognized Heinrich and therefore did not know whose brave assault had saved him. He galloped up to his tent, quickly dismounted, and sat down angrily on his throne. The princes all came at once and crowded around him. "You see, my lords," said the emperor, "how I was nearly betrayed. But for two knightly hands that came to my aid, I would have been killed. If I knew who gave me such bold succor—freeing me although naked—I would present him with gifts and fiefs, for I owe my life to his help. Indeed there never was a finer, bolder knight. For God's sake, whoever knows him must bring him to me: I promise before you all that he will receive a rich reward. Truly, my heart is—and always will be—well disposed toward him. There is no other knight living who is so excellent, here or elsewhere."

Some of those standing there knew that it was Heinrich who had rescued the emperor and they all cried out together: "Lord, we know the warrior who saved your most precious life, but, sad to say, he now bears the heavy burden of your disfavor. It is his misfortune to have so acted as to lose your good will. If he should be lucky enough to regain it, we would show him to you."

"Had he slain my own father," replied the emperor, "I would pardon him and grant him my favor. I promise it on my word and on my imperial honor." When they told him it was Heinrich von Kempten, the great emperor said quickly, "If he is in this country, I can readily believe you. Who else would have fought stark naked, as the man did today, but a knight whose heart is so bold that he dared to drag an emperor over a table by the beard? He has a brave and reckless spirit but he will never suffer because of it, for my favor will always protect him. However I shall receive him angrily and give him a scare."

The monarch gave orders that Heinrich be brought at once to his court, and the knight soon was sternly led before him. Assuming a hostile manner, the mighty emperor then said, "Tell me, how do you dare follow me down here and appear before my eyes? You know very well why I became your enemy. You are the one who trimmed my beard without a razor; your fierce rage robbed it of so much hair that it still has no curl. You did that. Your presuming to come to this country shows that you are deliberately being haughty and arrogant."

"Pardon, my lord," said the warrior. "I ask you to forgive my coming here, since I was forced to do so. My lord, one of the princes present commanded me to accompany him, whatever the danger, if I wished to keep his favor. I now declare, and pledge my soul's salvation, that I did not want to make the journey: as God is my witness, I came only at my lord's express order. Had I forgone the expedition and not set out with him, he would have taken my fief from me."

The emperor then laughed and said, "You are a fine man. I know that you are innocent and therefore shall gladly put aside my wrath toward you. I welcome you with God a thousand times. You rescued me from great distress and saved my life, for I would have died without your help, good man." With this he sprang up, ran to the knight, and kissed his eyes and hands. They were thus happily reconciled and made their peace: enmity vanished, because the emperor was no longer angry at Heinrich. He gave him money and a fief that brought in two hundred marks a year. The knight's strength and bold courage therefore made him very rich and so highly esteemed that he is still remembered today. For this reason let every knight cast aside all cowardice, be proud of his bravery, and use his strength. Valor and knightly deeds have become quite rare, but they still bring fame and honor to everyone who can practice them and live as they demand.

Here the account closes and so also does this short tale that I took from Latin and put into German verse at the request of the Lord of Diersburg. It was composed in the good city of Straßburg where he is cathedral provost and a bright flower of great esteem. May God increase his blessings in keeping with his many virtues. I, Konrad von Würzburg, shall always pray for his welfare: he has striven for honor with a generous hand. This is the end of the work.

Laurin

THERE ONCE LIVED in Verona a brave warrior named Dietrich, the like of whom was not to be found in those days: he was so bold that no one dared to oppose him in battle, and he never did anything shameful. He was a model prince, whose vassals were the best men in the country. These nobles who took care of his land abhorred infamy and disgrace and never neglected honor and valor. Wherever they were, they were always praising the lord of Verona above all others.

"I don't know a man on earth who lives so commendably as the noble Dietrich," said Wieland's son, an able and valiant knight. "Nowhere can one find his equal, a warrior who has done such great things. He deserves greater acclaim than anybody else."

"He knows nothing about the adventure in the hollow mountains that are guarded by the dwarfs," replied the old Master Hildebrand. "One must admit that whoever wants to see their wonders learns to know fear and distress: they have killed many warriors. He has never endured the danger there. When he conquers them, I'll maintain that he excels all the rest."

Meanwhile the lord of Verona had come up and heard what both had said. "Master Hildebrand of Garda, wise warrior," he spoke, "if your tale were true, you would have told it to me long ago."

This angered Hildebrand, and he rebuked the highborn prince: "He who wants to be well regarded, should keep his tidings to himself until he sees how they will be received. Thus he shows good breeding and will be honored. I know a little man who can do many wondrous things. He is hardly three spans tall, but he has cut hand and foot off of many who truly were larger than three of him. Then he freed them from all their cares. He is Laurin, a famous king and the boldest of men. The dwarfs are subject to him, for he rules all the wild lands. In Tirol he has raised himself a rose garden with great care and has placed a silk thread around it instead of a wall. Laurin avenges himself quickly on the one who breaks it and exacts a heavy fine: he takes his right foot and his left hand."

"He is a mighty warrior," said Dietrich of Verona, "but if I have a friend who will risk it with me, I will seek out the red roses even though this may lead me into great danger." Then the warrior Witege spoke up: "I must venture the journey with you, my dear lord, and be your companion to the garden where we can expect the adventure. As soon as I see the garden, I'll trample it all down."

The hunters then rode forth on a knightly undertaking. One was the esteemed Dietrich, his comrade was the brave Sir Witege, and they were riding to the forest of Tirol to hunt. After they had entered the forest and ridden on for seven leagues, they came to a green meadow in front of a rose garden. The little Laurin had adorned the rose bushes ornately, with gold, gold ribbon, and jewels. No one could tire of looking at the garden: it was delightful and drove away all sadness. The roses gleamed brightly and gave off a fragrant odor, which soon brought them to grief.

"My dear friend Witege," said the lord of Verona politely, "this is surely the garden of which Hildebrand told us. I am afraid that we shall be in real peril because, as far as I can judge, it is cared for by an able man. The roses send out a sweet smell day and night. I could never get too much of them if we were allowed to stay in there."

"Even if it is the devil who tends it, by black magic," replied Witege, "I must lessen his pride in the garden. Get down from your horse." They dismounted onto the green grass, and Witege at once cut down the roses: the golden ribbons were trampled in the dirt and the jewels no longer gleamed. We have heard that the joy and splendor of the garden was destroyed. The blooms lost their fragrance and bright beauty, which pained them greatly. Then the warriors sat on the grass and forgot their troubles. However the thread had been broken, and this brought vengeance on them.

Look! A fierce dwarf named Laurin came riding up. In his hand he held a spear fit for a ruling prince. The shaft was wound with gold, and near the head fluttered a silk banner which displayed two greyhounds, running swiftly as if chasing fleet game in a wild forest. They appeared to be alive when the banner whipped in the wind. His horse was the size of a roe and spotted on the sides. It wore a golden saddle cloth with jewels that shone like the sun in the shadow of the forest. The rein which the little Laurin held in his hand when he found the two princes was red gold. His saddle was of ivory, and its bow sparkled with the many rubies set in it. The stirrups in which he stood in a knightly manner were very costly; his leg armor was blood-red, and no sword was good enough to cut into it.

The dwarf had a very fine cuirass. It shown brightly with gold, had been hardened in dragon's blood, and could not be conquered by the sharpest sword: it was skillfully wrought. Around it was a magic belt that gave him the strength of twelve men, so he was always the victor. At his side hung a sword with which he had fought many battles. It was a span wide and could cut through iron, steel, and stone; the hilt was of gold, and a jacinth gleamed brightly from the pommel. The sword was worth more than a country. His surcoat which he always wore in battle, was made of seventy-two pieces of different kinds of silk and sparkled with precious stones.

Laurin's helmet was of red gold in which a carbuncle and many rubies were set:

no night was ever so dark but that these jewels would make it as bright as day. On the helmet was a golden crown such as God himself might desire, and on the crown were birds—conceived with cunning and fashioned with magic—that sang sweetly and looked in every respect as if they were alive. He had a gold-trimmed shield that had never been damaged by a spear. It displayed a golden leopard which appeared alive and about to spring on another wild beast.

The princes waited while Laurin approached. As soon as he came near enough for them to see him clearly, Witege exclaimed, "God protect us! My dear friend Dietrich, that may well be an angel, the wise St. Michael, who has ridden from paradise."

"I am glad to see the angel," replied the lord of Verona. "However you had better tighten your helmet, because I am afraid he is angry at us: if this is his meadow, he has a good right to be."

When the dwarf was within speaking distance, the princes started to greet him, but he interrupted them in a rage: "Who told you madmen to dismount in this clearing and hobble your nags on my green meadow that I have guarded and defended from so many fools? You will pay a heavy penalty! Who asked you donkeys to come here? You will suffer dearly for having trampled my lovely red roses! Each of you shall give me his right foot and left hand."

"No, no, little man," answered Dietrich courteously, "Don't be angry. One shouldn't exact feet and hands from princes who can pay you well with silver and gold. In May when God sends the joys of summer, many other roses will blossom. I tell you truly that it is not fitting to punish princes by taking their hands and feet. I don't want to forfeit them when I have such great wealth."

Laurin went on without restraint. "I have more gold than three of you," he said. "What kind of princes are you? If you are two noblemen, your actions do not show it. What did you avenge by destroying my rose garden and trampling my golden ribbons in the dirt? I have done you no harm. If I had, you should have sent a challenge and attacked me because of it. That would have been princely behavior."

"Do you hear him, Sir Dietrich?" exclaimed the bold son of Wieland. "You have never acted like this: listening to such talk when you are a worthy king. As simple as the little fellow is, he still displays great arrogance and tells us what he intends to do. If you approve, sir, I'll take him by the feet and beat him against the side of the hill."

"God does wonders," replied the lord of Verona. "What if he has done one with him? If this little man didn't know that he was strong and able, he wouldn't have spoken to us so haughtily. I tell you truly that him whom God has honored the world too will always faithfully honor in many ways, which is right. Now take my advice here on this meadow: be valiant, but not overly so. He who wants to be highly regarded should act as if he did not hear that which disturbs him and should let it pass until he is in real danger. Then let him show what he can do, and he will remain without reproach in any land."

Incensed by these words, Witege upbraided the prince: "Anyone who calls you a brave man and proven warrior is indeed a liar. If you are afraid of that little man over there by the rock, you couldn't frighten a mouse. You don't believe that you can protect yourself against him when one of us could destroy three thousand or more of such creatures. Either you or I would seem to him like an army, for he rides a horse that, God knows, is no larger than a goat. I would dare to fight a thousand of him." Thus spoke the mighty man.

"You think you are fierce, Sir Witege," said Laurin. "Indeed you think you are the devil himself, but one can fight you and live through it. I have an especial hatred for you, so, since you are such an able man, you shall face me first. Tighten your saddle girths, and the breaststrap too if you think this needs it, for we shall have a joust that an emperor would be glad to see."

The bold Witege dismounted and tightened the girths—you can be sure of that—and he did think it well to adjust the breaststrap. Then he sprang into the saddle without touching the stirrups, which Laurin applauded. They tied on their helmets at once and dashed at each other like falcons on the wing. One was large, the other—Laurin of the short legs—was small. Witege missed, and the little dwarf knocked him to the ground: the prince had never felt so ashamed.

Laurin dismounted to collect a heavy fine, the right foot and the left hand, and would have done so if the lord of Verona had not intervened. Dietrich thought the penalty too severe and extended his sword over Witege. "No, Laurin," he said. "Spare the warrior for my sake. He is my companion, as everyone may know, and came with me. If he were to suffer such a punishment, I would be disgraced wherever this was told about the lord of Verona. It would be a painful story for me."

"What is your fame to me?" answered Laurin. "The lord of Verona, you say? I have heard much about you and am glad you have come. You shall pay me the same forfeit: the right foot and the left hand. I'll show you my strength and skill. You broke down my garden, trampled roses and ribbons in the dirt, and you shall suffer for it. However small I seem to you, I would defeat you if there were an army of one or even three thousand of you."

Dietrich said no more. He went to his horse and jumped into the saddle without using the stirrups, which Laurin applauded. He intended to knock the dwarf from his horse and was just taking his spear in hand in knightly fashion when his mentor Hildebrand appeared, and with him the berserker Wolfhart, who never missed a fight, and Sir Dietleib of Styria. The dwarf was to bring them all into danger.

"My dear Dietrich," the wise Hildebrand called to his lord, "hear this. If you don't listen to my advice, you will be dishonored. You don't know the dwarf: you can't joust with him. If all the world supported you, he would still unhorse you. You would thus lose your renown and, able as you are, would not presume to remain a ruling prince. I counsel you, bold warrior, to dismount and fight him on foot; this is my best advice. And keep one thing in mind: you cannot get to him through his splendid armor, for no blade will cut it. Use your strength in another way. Strike him around the ears with the hilt until he is crazed. Unless God forsakes you, you will defeat him in this manner."

Dietrich did not fail to do as his mentor counseled. He dismounted and said fiercely, "I challenge you, Laurin. Now avenge your injury on me."

"Indeed I shall, sir," answered Laurin. Seizing his shield, he then ran at the lord of Verona and gave him such a mighty blow that the latter's shield fell to the ground. Enraged, Dietrich charged at Laurin and struck the edge of his shield so hard that it flew from his hand. Since he could not defeat the dwarf with skill, Sir Dietrich tried to stun him, as Hildebrand had advised. With his sword hilt he struck the little Laurin with such force on the helmet that it and the golden crown resounded for half a league. The dwarf lost his daring and didn't know where he was. He reached into his pouch, pulled out his magic cloak, and covered himself with it so that the lord of Verona could not see him. This caused the faithful prince great distress. He soon received many deadly wounds, and the blood ran down his cuirass.

"I'd strike you dead," said the lord of Verona, "but I don't know where you went or who took you from me. You just vanished from before my eyes." He swung at the dwarf in great wrath and made a cut a yard deep in a rock. Laurin then ran at him and struck him fiercely. In his great need Dietrich protected himself well with his sword, as skillful warriors do.

"I shall never cease to mourn if the dwarf kills you," the wise Hildebrand called to his lord. "Hold on to him if he should want to wrestle, for this might favor you. His magic cloak wouldn't help him then." To this Dietrich answered: "Could I wrestle with him, I might well do better." He was furious at the dwarf.

As soon as Laurin heard that the brave man wanted a wrestling match, he gave him one. He dropped his sword, ducked under that of his much larger opponent, and seized him so mightily about the knees that they both fell to the ground. The lord of Verona was greatly chagrined at this.

"Dietrich, my dear lord," cried Hildebrand again, "break his belt and you can defeat him. This gives him the strength of twelve men." It was a savage struggle that made the prince more and more angry the longer it lasted. Steam came from his mouth like fire from a forge, and all kindness left him. He picked up the dwarf by the belt and threw him to the earth with such force that the belt broke, which was unlucky for Laurin. It fell on the ground, Hildebrand picked it up, and the dwarf had lost the strength of twelve men. When Dietrich beat him against the earth in a rage, the splendid Laurin uttered a wail that resounded over hill and valley.

"If you ever were an upright man, be merciful!" he cried to Dietrich. "Spare my life, and I shall be subject to you with all that is mine." Laurin pled in vain, for the lord of Verona knew no mercy. He beat the dwarf against the earth so hard that the other warriors felt sorry for him. Then the little man called to Dietleib: "Help me, noble and dauntless knight of Styria! You owe me this, for your sister is my wife. Do honor to all noblewomen and save me!"

Dietleib did not delay, but ran to Dietrich. "Noble and esteemed lord of Verona," he exclaimed, "show your regard for all knights by giving Laurin to me." However Dietrich was without pity, and the entreaty did no good. The young man therefore called to the prince again: "If noblewomen are dear to you, give him to me."

"It is useless to appeal to me," replied the lord of Verona angrily, "for I won't give Laurin to you. He has caused me great distress and shall pay for it."

"No, no!" said Dietleib. "Give up your wrath for my sake, noble ruler of Verona, and I will gladly serve you and be subject to you the rest of my life." Dietleib's plea was in vain because of Dietrich's rage. "No one can help him," he said. "Even if it costs me your service, he will die."

The lord of Styria did not give up, but became very angry. He ran to his horse and, without touching the stirrups, sprang into the saddle with such force that his cuirass clanged loudly. He was a fierce man. He spurred his horse and rode to Dietrich in knightly manner. "Give me the little dwarf," he said, "if you value my good will." The lord of Verona did not reply, and Dietleib could easily see that he was still enraged. The young man therefore picked Laurin up by his bright cuirass, in spite of anything Dietrich could do, and rode with him across the heath.

The bold lord of Verona called to Hildebrand: "Have my horse brought to me. That dwarf treated me so shamefully that he can never make amends, and now he is about to escape." They led up his horse, and he mounted. He was filled with pain and wrath and had lost all kindness. "If the devil doesn't come from hell to save you," he raged, "I'll avenge my comrade."

Dietrich galloped across the heath, followed by Hildebrand, Witege, and Wolfhart. However, Dietleib was no coward. After he had hidden Laurin in the forest, he rode back toward them. When he saw the lord of Verona, he said politely: "I ask you in the name of all virtue to let me have the dwarf." However Dietrich would not listen to the appeal, because of his anger, but instead lowered his spear. Dietleib would not give way, and the two charged. They broke their spears on each other, and, dismounting, raised their shields before them and drew two sharp swords. The worthy princes ran at one another and began the greatest single combat ever seen before or since. Since the battle brought both of them painful wounds, they were furious at each other. They stamped their feet so hard that the earth came up over their spurs as mighty blows resounded on helmets. The sound of their swords was heard half a league away. The grim Dietleib ran at Dietrich and struck him such a blow that the shield flew from his hand. The lord of Verona had to retreat before the mighty warrior—he had no choice— and held out his sword for protection.

"Come on!" cried Hildebrand then. "We won't let them fight any longer. You two charge Dietleib." Witege and Wolfhart ran at the young man. They were both strong and, although he defended himself well, they threw him down at last and did not let him go until they had sheathed his sword. Hildebrand pulled his lord away, forced him to put up his sword, and made a peace that included Laurin, who then was no longer in the peril from which Dietleib had rescued him. After the two princes were reconciled, Dietleib rode off to get his brother-in-law. When he brought him back to the clearing, Witege and Dietrich glared fiercely at the dwarf: they still hated him for the distress he had caused them.

"Tell me," said Dietleib then to Laurin, "do you indeed have my sister? If so, I will accept you as a brother-in-law."

"Yes," replied Laurin, "I seized her openly on the morning of the day before yesterday. All of the time I was in danger I thought of her, my dearest wife. I tell you truly that she is now a noble queen to whom all the dwarfs are subject. You can believe me when I relate how I got her.

"Listen, bold warrior. I found the chaste and lovely creature near the castle of Styria under a linden to which she and many other pretty maidens had come for an outing. Two men were guarding her, but I stole her away from them with magic. I came riding up in knightly fashion, yet so that no one saw me or spoke to me. I rode under the linden and there caught sight of the beautiful maiden, who outshone the others as the moon outshines the stars. Her name is Lady Kühnhilde. I seized her by the hand, threw my cloak over her, and swung her up on the horse in front of me. Even though I carried her off by force, no one saw us. I took her with me into the mountain where many male and female dwarfs with gold and jewels wait on her.

"I tell you the truth: I have more wealth than all the kings together have, and it is all in her hands. I could pay for all the lands with gold and precious stones and still have enough to be called rich, enough to redeem three kingdoms. And everything I have is subject to her." Laurin then added, "Your sister is still a maiden."

Dietleib was pleased to hear all this. "I am glad I risked my life for you," he said. "Let me see my sister. If what you have told me is the truth, I would rather that you have her than anyone else."

"I'll show you that it is true," answered Laurin. "Now let us be friends."

Hildebrand led Dietrich aside and said, "My dear lord, you should be Dietleib's friend. He is indeed a mighty man and will stand by you faithfully. He could help you against anyone. This is my counsel."

"My dear mentor," replied Dietrich very politely, "I shall do whatever you advise." Then Hildebrand went to Dietleib and said, "Hear me, noble warrior. I tell you without deceit that it will be a great honor for you to have him as a comrade who is the lord of many warriors. I can say this truly."

"I have heard all about him," answered Dietleib, "and I agree. If he will show favor to my brother-in-law, I will be his friend."

"You have my word that he will," said Master Hildebrand of Garda. "We must all be comrades." Dietleib and Dietrich, two mighty men, then took an oath of friendship. The little Laurin was also included, just as if he were large and tall. This was only because of Dietleib, for Witege didn't like the dwarf. He was afraid that Laurin would make trouble for him.

"Now that we are all friends," declared Laurin, "I promise to put everything I have at your disposal. If you will come with me into the mountain, there will be many male and female dwarfs with gold and jewels to wait on you and much singing and stringed music to amuse you. Truly you will see so many beautiful things there that a year will seem a very short time. You must believe this, for it is no lie: I cannot tell you half of the delights in the mountain that shall be yours if you dare trust yourselves to me." The four princes took Hildebrand aside and asked the old warrior whether they should entrust themselves to the dwarf. "We shall follow your counsel," they said.

"If I knew the proper course for us, so that I could advise you," he answered, "I would gladly do so. Noble ruler of Verona, should we refuse out of fear, it truly would not look good. We would be dishonored wherever it was cited as an act of cowardice. It would be a disgrace for us."

"He who gave us our life can indeed protect it," said Sir Dietrich devoutly, "Let us rely on Him, for He can help us. I must see this adventure to the end, even though I should come to harm."

"The devil take the dwarf!" exclaimed Witege. "He wants to deceive us all with lies."

"Let's go," said the berserker Wolfhart. "We must see the beautiful things of which he told us." Then Hildebrand spoke to Laurin: "Hear me, little warrior. We will trust your word. See that you keep it."

"I shall stand by you faithfully as long as I live," he replied. "You can rely on me fully." They followed him therefore toward a hollow mountain, although Witege was opposed to this. The journey was to bring them into great danger.

When they first saw the wondrous mountain, it seemed close by, but they did not reach it until early the next morning. Then the bold warriors rode openly up to it and dismounted on a meadow under a linden tree. They turned their horses loose on the meadow, that was really delightful. It was covered with blossoms of every sort one could wish or imagine, and all gave off a lovely fragrance. The meadow was filled with every kind of songbird. It was marvelous: each sang splendidly—their throats resounded sweetly—and all of the voices rang out in harmony over the plain. Playing there were many types of beasts that had been tamed to friendliness and made native to that very field. I tell you truly that it contained many joys. Anyone who saw it would forget all his sorrows.

"My troubles are gone!" exclaimed the lord of Verona. "If my senses do not deceive me, we are in paradise."

"God sent us here," said Wolfhart, "so that we could tell those at home that we have had an unusual experience. Truly the meadow is filled with every delight."

"You should enjoy your senses," said Hildebrand, "and I am glad that you do so. But don't praise the day before the evening."

"If you listened to me and took my advice," spoke up Witege, "the little man wouldn't deceive us. He is so full of tricks that no one should trust him."

Then Laurin said, "You should enjoy the pleasures of this wondrous meadow without care. However the delights here are nothing compared with those inside the mountain. Whenever we want some fresh air, we come to this meadow. Each makes himself a garland, and we dance with many red-lipped maidens. Later all those outside go back into the mountain. Thus our life is always filled with pleasure. I will share this meadow with you, my friends," the little man continued. "It shall belong to us all."

"My troubles are over," thought Dietrich. However this was not so, God knows, for their joys soon vanished.

The princes left their horses on the meadow and went on, as Laurin led them into the mountain. When they came to the door, they saw standing there twelve beautiful maidens, who quickly greeted them. After they were all inside, the door was barred, and none was so wise that he knew where they were, or had sight so keen that he could see.

"I am not lying," said Witege, "if I were alone out there, the little man would never entice me in. That is the truth. I think we all have been betrayed."

"You don't need to worry," said Laurin, "for I won't harm you. I won't break my word."

Soon the princes saw many splendid knights approaching, dressed in the finest clothing—gleaming with gold—to be found anywhere. Dietrich and his friends were well received. Hanging above them, they saw great numbers of many types of gems: the mountain was filled with every kind of jewel in the world. Laurin ruled in grandeur with a large retinue of warriors. You may be sure that no king was ever so powerful but that they could have given him a good battle. The lives of all of them were devoted to bold deeds.

The noble guests saw many beautiful things and were treated very well. They were seated on golden benches that sparkled with precious stones, and the best of wine and mead was poured for them. There was much entertainment of different kinds for them to watch. On one side there was singing; on the other men were jumping and engaged in tests of strength; then came the spear throwing and stone throwing, with several events going on at the same time; riders charged into each other right in front of them, and many spears were broken in jousts; they heard a large number of skillful musicians: fiddlers, harpers, and pipers.

Later two short fiddlers, delightful dwarfs in rich and elegant clothing, came before the princes. The fiddles they carried were of red gold, glittered with jewels, and were worth more than a country. Their strings made sweet music. The princes enjoyed the fiddling, and time passed quickly.

"I like the entertainment," said the lord of Verona. "This mountain is full of joys." Afterwards two fine singers and narrators appeared and sang many courtly tales to amuse and charm the guests. Their lovely voices resounded through the mountain. Anyone who was well-versed in song would have forgotten all his sorrow.

At last Queen Kühnhilde came forth and with her many beautiful female dwarfs who wore costly silk clothing and the finest jewelry to be made from silver, gold, and precious stones. It all looked splendid on them. The queen had on a golden crown that could not have been bought with a kingdom. She gave a friendly greeting to the stately guests.

"Welcome, worthy prince, noble Dietrich of Verona!" she said. "I am glad to see you, for I have heard tell of your notable virtues and of the many great deeds of bravery you have performed without defeat. You have never done anything shameful and deserve to be praised above all men." Dietrich thanked her.

She greeted the others in like manner, as warmly as she could and in keeping with her station. She welcomed Dietleib especially. She put her arms around him, pressed him to her breast, and kissed him. Indeed she embraced him so fondly that he could not fail to pity her when the beautiful maiden lamented her sorrow.

"Dear sister," he said, "do you want to stay in this hollow mountain with the little dwarf, or would you rather leave him? You can surely get another husband."

"Bless you, dear brother!" she replied. "I lack nothing, as you can see. If I ask for one of something, I get four; and my heart is gladdened when I look at the mountain and all my maidens. Nevertheless I am sad. I do not like this life because these people are heathen, and since they do not believe in God, their works are not fitting for me. I would rather be among Christians, but I will entrust myself to your faithfulness and do as you advise."

"My lovely sister," replied the bold Dietleib, "I'll take you away from the dwarf if it costs me my life."

When Laurin bade the lords come to the table, they took off their armor and put on fine silk clothing, adorned with gold and jewels, which the dwarf had supplied to honor them. The food was then placed before them. They were served enough of everything good to eat—their host was better able to do this than any king—and still there was plenty more. His plates were of silver; the pitchers gleamed brightly of gold and precious stones; his table was of ivory with gold at the joints, that were as smooth as if they had been cast. After they had eaten and drunk and the tables had been cleared, the princes sat there and listened to the singing and recitation that was performed before them. This was followed by music from so many stringed instruments that the entire mountain resounded. A throng of merry dwarfs thus began the entertainment anew.

Meanwhile Laurin had gone to Kühnhilde. "My dear wife," he said, "may you evermore be blessed! Give me your loyal advice, for my plight is grievous. Let me tell you what these warriors have done to me. Although I have never harmed them, they destroyed my garden and trampled the golden ribbons in the dirt. I would have gotten revenge for this if my belt had not broken. Because of Dietrich's anger, I am now disgraced. Should Dietleib not take their part, it ought to cost them their lives."

"You would never live it down," answered the queen. "Warrior, consider your honor and follow my counsel. Punish them in such a way that they will let you alone. But you must give me your word that you won't kill anyone."

The dwarf promised her this. On his right hand he then placed a wondrous golden ring with a jewel that made him very strong—he got the strength of twelve men—and sent for Dietleib. The warrior at once came to the chamber where he was.

"My dear brother-in-law," said Laurin, "I'll share all I have with you if you won't side with your companions."

"I would rather die," replied Dietleib. "Whatever happens to them must happen to me. I don't need your wealth."

"In that case you will have to stay in here," said Laurin, "until you change your mind and are glad to accept my gift." The dwarf was very cunning and was able to lock up his brother-in-law in the room. This done, he hurried back to the four princes. It is said that he had mead and wine brought them to which, by his order, a narcotic had been added: soon after they drank it, they sank down on the benches. The little warrior quickly tied all four of them together and threw them into a dungeon, where they suffered great distress. Were it not for Dietrich's anger, they would have been lost.

Now they were captives. How will they escape? They never will unless the story teller is given a drink.

Not long after the dwarf had imprisoned them by treachery in the mountain, the lords realized that they were bound. This made Dietrich so angry that his mouth gave off fumes hot enough to burn away his bonds. He freed his feet and hands and then released his suffering friends. However they did not know how to get good armor, for it was locked up and well guarded by the wild dwarfs. Thus they remained there in misery until the fourth morning.

In order to help the warriors, Kühnhilde had the precious stones in the mountain covered over so that their light was hidden: since they could not see, everyone else went back to bed. She, however, hurried to the room where Dietleib was and unlocked the door. When he sprang out in a rage, she said, "Bless you, my dear brother! If you don't follow my counsel, you will lose both life and honor."

"Dearest sister," he replied, "I'll do whatever you advise. Now tell me truly how my friends are. Are they alive, or dead, or in some sort of distress?"

"They are prisoners deep in a dungeon where they are suffering great hardships," said Kühnhilde. "I pity them."

"If I had my good armor on and my sword in hand," exclaimed Dietleib, "I would free them at once."

"Bless you, brother!" she answered. "If you were four times as strong as you are, the dwarfs would quickly beat you down so that you would have to admit defeat, for you can't see them. Here, put this ring on your finger and you will observe something wondrous. I assure you that you will then be able to see them very well." The warrior was indeed pleased when she slipped it on his finger, because he now could see the dwarfs.

"If I had my cuirass and sword," he said, "a lot of dwarfs would suffer for this. I would kill them, females as well as males, and not spare a one. It is a treacherous race."

Kühnhilde took him by the hand and led him straight to a room where they found all the lords' armor, gleaming with gold, even though it had been hidden from them. The queen stealthily helped the warrior put on his armor and tied his helmet on his head. In his hands she placed his sword—that was worth more than a kingdom—and his gold-trimmed shield, on which a very life-like sea monster played.

"Listen, dear brother," she said. "Watch out for Laurin! If he defeats you, it will be the death of all of us."

"Unless the devil from bitter hell aids him," answered Dietleib, "I shall free my comrades."

To help him the worthy lady made the sign of the cross over the warrior many times and said, "May God care for you and preserve your life. Now look, they carried your friends to the cellar and put them into a dungeon where they lie in great distress." When he heard this, Dietleib picked up their armor and their fine swords—each worth a kingdom—took them to the cellar, and dropped them before his friends with a clang that resounded throughout the mountain.

Pained and angered, Laurin called up all his retinue by sounding a loud bugle call that all the dwarfs could hear. It was followed by a jingling of fine mail being put on in haste, as if they were eager to join the battle. The dwarfs appeared before their king very quickly: three thousand or more, so we have heard.

"Don't let any of them live," ordered Laurin. "Their faith is a false one, for they do not trust us." Then a huge throng began to crowd toward the cellar where the stout-hearted Dietleib was standing. He was a true warrior and could see the dwarfs well. As they pressed toward him, the youth sprang about among them, swung his sword so fast that one could feel the breeze, and killed a large number. It was child's play for him. Laurin was furious when he saw the great damage done to him. He charged at Dietleib and quickly gave him so many deep wounds that the blood ran down his mail. Dietleib had a good sword with which he had cut through hard helmets in many battles, but it did not help him now, for it could not wound Laurin.

I tell you truly that there were many dwarfs in the mountain and all were attacking one man. He began to fight more fiercely—a single blow that he swung behind him killed many dwarfs—but his efforts were in vain, and they pressed the young man back into the cellar. Meanwhile the wise Hildebrand quickly led his companions out of the dungeon, and they put on their armor. If Dietleib had not been defending the entrance to the cellar, the dwarfs could have killed them without harm to themselves. Now they were trying to drive the youth out of the way. However he fought mightily, and many dwarfs died as the four warriors hastily armed themselves.

"I have never been so eager to fight as now!" exclaimed the lord of Verona. "But though this mountain is full of battle, I can't see anyone and can't tell whom to strike and whom to help."

"My lord," said Hildebrand, "I'll give you something that is worth more than a country. I'd rather you had the honor than I myself. Take this belt. I tell you truly that you will see the dwarfs clearly as soon as you put it around you." He placed the belt in his hand, and the warrior girded it on. His heart was filled with joy because he could now see all the dwarfs. He also saw the peril of Dietleib, who was extending his sword to ward off the enemy as his armor reddened with blood.

"My dear comrades," said Dietrich, "stay here in the cellar. You can't see our foes and could easily be harmed. I never saw such a large army as this host of dwarfs. They are wounding Dietleib: his armor is red with blood. He will be killed if I don't help him."

"Hear my advice," said Hildebrand. "On his right hand Laurin has a ring that gives him his strength. Cut the finger off and bring it quickly to me."

"Master Hildebrand," replied Dietrich politely, "if I see him, I'll cut it from his hand and bring it to you at once." He ran to the entrance of the cellar, and was quickly set upon by a great throng of fierce dwarfs. Laurin too charged at him, which pleased Dietrich. He cleared a wide space about himself, drove back the attackers, and would let no one in. However he received many wounds through his cuirass, so we have heard, from the host of dwarfs.

When neither cunning nor anger enabled him to defeat Laurin, the prince sprang at him with unrestrained fury. The steam from Dietrich's mouth then was so hot that sweat poured from the dwarf's mail. The mighty man truly hated Laurin. He made a feint that Hildebrand had taught him and, to his enemy's dismay, cut off the finger that wore the ring. He snatched it up and gave it to Hildebrand—who was delighted, for now he too could clearly see all the dwarfs.

Meanwhile a dwarf had run out of the mountain. In anger and distress he loudly sounded a horn that was heard at once by five giants in the forest. Without delay they ran up to the mountain, steel rods in hand, and asked the dwarf what was wrong.

"These men are too fierce for us," he replied, "I can't tell you half of what they have done. My lord's retinue has been badly beaten and he himself defeated. Come and help him!" The giants crowded into the mountain, to the joy of the dwarfs. Those who had hidden in fear sprang forth and ran to help the giants and those who before had fled now fought boldly again. The frightful giants then attacked the two men.

"I advise you to remain here in the cellar," said Hildebrand to the others, "for a second great battle is beginning. I see five terrible giants who have come to help the dwarfs. They have set upon our friends, and I must go to their aid." Witege and Wolfhart fretted impatiently. They heard the fierce assault of the giants on their comrades, but could not see how the battle was going.

"Wolfhart, my friend," exclaimed Wieland's son, "are we, who never avoided a fight in our lives, to be cowards now?"

"Let's go!" cried the berserker Wolfhart. "We'll push forward together to where we hear the battle taking place and then rush in with swords swinging. That is my counsel." They had just tied on their helmets and snatched up their shields when—look—there came Kühnhilde.

"You are two stalwart men," she said, "just as I have heard. I must praise your bravery in wanting to fight, even though you cannot see the enemy, and shall reward you." She gave each a ring and continued, "Put them on your fingers and something wondrous will happen to you: truly, you will be able to see all of your foes." They slipped them on and were filled with joy, for a wonder did indeed occur: they could clearly see the dwarfs. Witege and his companion bowed to the noble queen, seized their shields, and sprang out of the cellar. Many dwarfs, and also the fearful giants, were to suffer because of them.

The strides of the two bold men were long, and their hauberks jingled loudly as they rushed to the battle, for they were eager to fight. Nagelring and Mimming were dreadful. The edges of these swords did not spare the dwarfs and showed no mercy. Sparks flew as if the swords were on fire as the two warriors dealt out many wounds. They reached their comrades without mishap, and then all five fell on the giants. Each chose one, and they soon gave them such deep wounds that the princes were wading in blood up over their spurs. The giants would gladly have been elsewhere but could find no way to escape from the warriors and—so we are told—were all killed. Laurin was then captured, and the battle was over.

When the dwarf viewed the harm done by the warriors and saw that they intended to kill everyone in the mountain, he fell down before Dietrich in great sorrow. "Noble and mighty prince," he cried, "show me your kindness! I have yielded myself to your mercy: do not let all my people be slain. Be generous to me and all of them will serve you. Stop the fighting quickly, noble prince, before the entire army of helpless dwarfs is destroyed."

"You will die," replied Dietrich angrily, "you and all your subjects. You broke faith with me and shall pay for it." This was heard by the beautiful Kühnhilde who was nearby. She went at once to the lord of Verona and said, "Noble Sir Dietrich, honor all women by granting me a favor that I request most urgently. For my sake, don't kill Laurin and his retinue, but give them a reprieve."

"Indeed we cannot let the dwarfs live," answered Dietrich politely. "They must die for the grief they have caused me."

"No, no, mighty prince! Act toward me according to your courtesy. Do not disappoint me, but do as I desire. Let me also profit by your virtues, that are so highly praised."

"I must counsel you to grant the maiden her wish," spoke up Hildebrand. "Let Laurin be your prisoner in Verona and have the dwarfs swear to serve you and place the mountain at your disposal."

"You should show good manners," said Dietleib, "and do as my sister entreats you."

"So be it," said Dietrich. "Maiden, your petition is granted." Then he called to Witege and Wolfhart: "Cease fighting and let the people live. I have promised them peace."

They broke off the conflict—it was none too soon—and the four princes considered their departure. They decided to take Laurin with them, together with a great deal of gold and jewels as booty, and agreed to entrust the hollow mountain to the loyalty of a highborn dwarf named Sintram. He was a worthy king, the second after Laurin, and he swore an oath of fealty to Dietrich.

The mighty princes and the beautiful maiden rode happily off to Verona, where they were welcome and had a friendly reception. There was much entertainment here and all sorts of pleasures. Dietleib and his sister remained for two weeks and passed the time joyfully. They then wished to depart and went to take leave of Dietrich. Kühnhilde asked the prince to reward her for what she had done for him.

"Remember, noble lord," she said, "the truth is that all of you would have died without Laurin's being harmed in the least. I feel guilty about this, because he treated me very well, gave me everything I desired, and placed all his possessions at my disposal. I therefore politely request, mighty prince, that you grant the petition which I shall present."

"Maiden," replied Dietrich courteously, "whatever you desire of me, you shall receive."

"I want something, noble prince, that you should grant me. Let me commend Laurin to your good will and mercy. Try to get him to receive baptism, treat him kindly afterwards, and—for my sake—restore him to his former position. You have indeed taught him not to break faith with you."

"Maiden, I shall be glad to do as you request," answered Dietrich graciously. At this Kühnhilde took leave of him in a courtly manner and went to where Laurin was.

"May God care for you, dear sir," she said. "I can't help it: I must go with my brother."

"Oh that I ever knew you!" exclaimed Laurin. "My faithfulness to you has gone for nothing. I wish I had never been born! I chose you to make me happy, and now my joyful days are past. If it were in my power, I would give all I ever owned to have you as my wife." He cried out so bitterly that Kühnhilde began to weep. Her brother then led her away from Verona and later gave her in marriage to a fine nobleman. She had many joys throughout the rest of her life.

Let them now set out happily while we turn back to Laurin and tell of his life and affairs.

"Sir," said Hildebrand, "you must act wisely with regard to the dwarf and begin carefully so that no one may learn what Lady Kühnhilde requested or that you are now his protector. He must be well guarded until his views are known: one must determine first of all if he will turn to a Christian life. He should be placed in the charge of the wise and esteemed Ilsung, who can care for and advise him so that he may truly become a Christian. Then you may pardon him." Following this counsel, Dietrich ordered that Laurin be kept under guard but entrusted to the wise man, who was to tell him about Christianity.

The dwarf would not become converted until after he had endured a great deal of insulting behavior from the youths there, who ridiculed him and made him the butt of many foolish jokes. When he had listened to this mockery for twelve weeks, he thought to himself, "If it will do me any good, I should become a Christian. I can indeed see that Christ's name is mighty on earth and that bands of angels serve Him, while my gods are blind and useless to me. My misfortune shows that He may well be powerful and that they cannot help me. Their aid was nothing when I cried to them in my distress, so I shall give them up and rely on a god called Jesus Christ who rules heaven and earth."

Early one Sunday morning while people were still sleeping, Laurin went to Ilsung and said, "Noble warrior, advise me as to how I may become a Christian and gain the favor of the prince."

"I'll give you counsel that will serve you well with both God and your lord," replied Ilsung, "and shall get full permission for you to do as you wish." He then went to Dietrich and told him what Laurin had said. The prince was pleased and had the dwarf brought before him.

"Now tell me the truth," he said. "Do you want to accept Christianity? If you do this willingly and without any false pride, God will reward you with an eternal crown."

"Sir," replied Laurin, "I am ready to receive of my own free will the blessing that the god of the Christians has given."

Dietrich sent at once for Hildebrand and others of his vassals. When they had come before him, a chaplain was summoned to consecrate the baptism, and a throng of happy courtiers gathered. The prince then asked them, "Advise me as to what name we should give him that would be suitable for a Christian."

"He need not be ashamed to keep his present name," they all answered. "Moreover, it is already well known everywhere." This counsel was taken, and the dwarf was baptized. Dietrich and Ilsung, who had helped convert him, were his sponsors. Afterwards Dietrich led Laurin into his great hall, summoned all his vassals, and said, "I shall do something today for my godson that will make his life happier. I shall swear to be his friend and protector and share life and wealth with him as long as he lives. He must also swear the same oath to me."

Laurin bowed down at his feet and, overcome with joy, was silent a long time. When Dietrich lifted him up, the dwarf said, "My lord, I will devote my life to keeping your favor." Then they took an oath of friendship. This relationship later became very close and lasted as long as they lived. Henceforth Laurin was treated with honor and was fully instructed in the way to serve God in the Faith. He learned it well.

Title page of *Helmbrecht* with an artist's conception of the hero.
Ambraser Heldenbuch, 225r, Austrian National Library, Ser. Nova 2665.

Helmbrecht

ONE PERSON TELLS of what he has seen, another of that which has happened to him, the third of love, the fourth of gain, the fifth of great possessions, and the sixth of high spirits. Here I shall relate my own experience: what I have seen with my own eyes and can assure you is true. Once I saw a farmer's son who had blond, curly hair that fell far down over his shoulders and wore a cap that was elegantly adorned with pictures. I don't believe anybody ever saw another cap with so many birds—parrots and doves—embroidered on it. Would you like to know what else was there?

There was a farmer called Helmbrecht, and it was his son of whom the story tells. They both had the same name, for the youth too was called Helmbrecht. I'll give you a short and simple account of the wonders depicted on the cap. (It can be trusted, for I am not guessing at anything.) From the hair at the back over the crown of his head to the lock in the middle of his forehead there was a border covered with birds that looked just as if they had flown there from the Spessart region. No peasant ever had a finer cap than that which Helmbrecht wore.

Do you want to hear what was embroidered by the right ear of this rustic fool? It was the story of how Troy was besieged after the bold Paris had stolen the Grecian king's wife (who was as dear to her husband as life itself), how towers and many stone walls fell when the city was conquered, and how Aeneas escaped to sea in his ships. It is too bad that a cap of which there is so much to tell should ever be worn by a peasant.

Now shall I tell you what was wrought in silk on the other side? On the left (this is no lie) appeared the mighty deeds performed by the four comrades in arms—Charlemagne, Roland, Turpin, and Oliver—in battle against the heathen. With bravery and cunning the king subdued Provence, Arles, and the land of Galicia, where formerly only heathen lived. And would you like to know what went from one ribbon to the other between his ears in back? I am telling you the truth: it was the story of how Lady Helche's sons and Diether of Verona were slain long ago by the fierce berserker Wittig in the fighting before Ravenna.

You surely want to learn about the other things the fool had on his cap, and I indeed know what was there. On the front border, from the right ear all around to the left—listen to this—was a dance scene such as one likes to see, embroidered in gleaming silk, with knights and ladies as well as youths and maidens. On one side each knight held two ladies by the hand (as is still done today) and on the other each youth danced between two maidens. Fiddlers were close by.

Listen to how the cap happened to be made for the forward and foolish Helmbrecht, for you haven't yet heard where it came from. It was sewn by a merry nun who had run away from her cell because she thought herself too pretty for a cloister. Her fate was that of many today: I have often seen women whose faces must blush because of what their bellies reveal. Helmbrecht's sister Gotelind had given a fine cow to the nun for her larder, and the latter, who was a skillful seamstress, repaid her by embroidering the cap and sewing clothing. Hear what his mother did when Gotelind gave this cow. She supplied the nun with more cheese and eggs than she had had during the entire time she had eaten at the cloister.

Besides the cap, Helmbrecht's sister provided him with lovely, white linen—no one ever wore better—so that he would be admired. It was so finely spun that seven weavers had run away from the loom before the cloth was finished. His mother moreover gave him a mantle (of the best wool ever cut by a tailor) with the whitest sheepskin lining in the country. Then the good woman got her dear son a mail doublet and a sword, which he surely deserved, and two other things he needed: a dagger and a large pouch. He who is so attired is considered arrogant even today.

After she had dressed him thus, the youth said, "Mother, I must have a jerkin too, for I would be quite disgraced without one. And it should be so made that you can tell yourself when you see it that your son will do you honor wherever he goes." In her chest she had a skirt which, sad to say, she now had to give up and exchange for some blue cloth to outfit her son. I swear that no farmer, here or elsewhere, ever had a jerkin which was even a little better than his. The one who advised him about it knew what was suitable and could show him how to gain high praise.

If you would like to hear more about the jerkin, I'll be glad to please you by describing it. There was a row of gilded buttons along the back, from the belt to the neck, and a row of silver-white buttons up to the clasp where the collar comes to the chin. There is no peasant between Hohenstein and Haldenberg who has taken such pains with a jacket or spent so much on one. How do you like this? In front were three crystal buttons, neither too large nor too small, with which the silly fool fastened the jerkin and also many others strewn about—yellow, blue, green, brown, red, black, and white—that gleamed afar just as he had wanted. When he went dancing, they glittered so brightly that he was regarded very fondly by both maidens and married women. I'll tell you the truth: beside this youth I would have made little impression on them. All around the seams where the sleeves were attached hung little bells that jingled loudly when he sprang about in the roundelay and resounded in the women's ears. If he were alive, Sir Neidhart could sing of it with his God-given talent better than I can tell it to you. At any rate you should know this: the mother sold many chickens and eggs before she could get him trousers and shoes.

After she had properly clothed his legs and feet, the vain youth said, "My dear father, I want to go to court and I need your help now. Mother and sister have given me so much that I shall be grateful to them as long as I live." His father was not pleased at this and replied sarcastically, "To go with your fine clothes I'll give you a fast horse that can leap hedges and ditches and run a long way without tiring. You need one at court, and I'll gladly buy it for you if I can find one cheap enough.

"Dear son, give up this journey. Courtly life is hard for those who have not grown up with it. You lead the team while I plow or I'll lead it while you plow, and together we'll cultivate the field. You will thus go to your grave with honor just as I shall do, or at least expect to. I am faithful and dependable—I never deceive anyone—and I pay my full tithe every year, as is right. I have lived without hate or enmity."

"Say no more, dear father," answered the youth. "It cannot be otherwise, for I must indeed get a taste of court life. Moreover I shall never again carry your sacks on my shoulders or pitch manure on your wagon, and may God's anger strike me if I ever yoke your oxen again or sow your oats. Truly that would not be in keeping with my long, blond hair and curly locks, my fine clothing, and my elegant cap with the silk doves that ladies have embroidered on it. I'll never again help you till the fields."

"Do stay with me," said the father. "I know that Farmer Ruprecht will give you his daughter and with her many sheep and swine and ten head of cattle, old as well as young. At court you will be hungry, will have to sleep on the bare floor, and will have no one to help you. Now take my advice, for it will bring you profit and honor. No one succeeds who does not accept his station, and yours is that of the plow; there are enough courtiers as it is. I swear to you by God, my dear son, that you will suffer disgrace and become the laughing stock of all those who really belong at court. You must listen to me and give up this plan."

"Father, I am certain that, with a horse to ride, I shall do as well with the manners of the court as those who have always been there. Whoever sees the beautiful cap on my head will swear a thousand oaths that I never led a team for you or guided a plow in a furrow. When I dress in the clothes that my mother and sister gave me yesterday, I surely shall not look at all as if I had once threshed out grain on a barn floor or set posts. As soon as I have put on the trousers and the shoes of Cordovan leather, nobody will suspect that I ever made a fence for you or anyone else. If you give me the horse, Farmer Ruprecht will never have me as a son-in-law, for I'll not relinquish my desires because of a woman."

"Be still a moment, my son, and listen to what I tell you. He who follows wise instruction gains wealth and respect, but the child who constantly ignores a father's counsel will finally come to shame and harm. If you really try to put yourself on the level of the wellborn courtier, you will fail, and he will become your enemy. And believe me, no peasant will complain about any injustice done you there. If a real courtier should seize all the property of a peasant, he would in the end do better in court than you. Listen to this, my son: if you take from the peasant just a little fodder for your horse and he gets the upper hand, then you are liable for everything that others have stolen from him. You won't get a chance to defend yourself, but will pay at once, for God is on his side if he kills you during the robbery. Believe what I say, dear son. Stay here and take a wife."

"No matter what happens to me, father, I'll not give up my plan, for I must win a higher position. Have your other sons labor with the plow. Cows shall low before me as I seize and drive them off. I have remained here this long only because I have no horse. Indeed, I am sorry that I am not galloping away with the other knights, pulling peasants through hedges by the hair. I can't bear poverty. When I can raise only one colt or calf in three years, the profit seems very small to me. I want to ride out for plunder every day so that I can live well and be safe from winter's cold as long as people will buy cattle. Hurry, father, don't delay but give me the horse at once, for I'll not stay any longer with you."

I'll be brief. To get the horse the father gave up four good cows, two oxen, three bulls, four bushels of grain, and twenty yards of rough woolen cloth—the longest piece of such fabric ever woven, so we are told. All gone for nothing! He bought the horse for ten pounds and could not have sold it the same day for three. Seven pounds lost!

Listen to what the son said when he dressed and was ready to leave. He shook his head, looked over one shoulder then the other, and exclaimed: "I am fierce enough to bite through stone. I could eat iron. The emperor himself should feel lucky if I don't lead him away captive and extort from him all he has, right down to his skin. And the same goes for the duke and several counts too. I'll trot across the fields and through the world with no fear for my life. Father, let me be my own master so that, from now on, I can grow up as I will. You could raise a wild Saxon more easily than me."

"All right, son, I release you from my keeping. Go your own way. But since the training I gave you means less than your curls, take care that no one touches your cap and the silk doves or harms your long, blond hair. If you really want no more of my instruction, I am sorely afraid that in the end you will walk with a crutch and go where a child leads you.

"My dear boy," continued the father, "let me yet dissuade you. You should live from that on which I live and from what your mother gives you. Drink water rather than wine gotten through robbery. Here in Austria everyone, foolish and wise, considers our bread to be fit for a king. You should eat it, dear son, instead of trading a plundered cow to some house-holder for a hen. Your mother makes a very fine soup that she cooks for a week. Stuff yourself with that and don't buy a goose with a plundered horse. Son, if you live as I have advised, you will be respected wherever you go, mix rye and oats rather than eat fish to your shame.

This is your father's teaching, and you would be wise to follow it. If you will not, then go your own way. I want no part of whatever wealth or fame you may win, and you also need not share your misfortune."

"You drink water, father, while I drink wine. And you can eat oatmeal while I have boiled chicken: no one will ever stop me. Moreover I shall never again eat any bread but wheat rolls until I die. Oat bread is for people like you. A Roman law book says that a young child takes on a trait of its godfather. Mine was a noble knight. God bless him for giving me such a proud spirit and causing me to become so noble."

"Believe me," said the father, "I would much prefer a man who always did what was right. Even were he of low birth, he would please everyone better than a man of royal blood who was worthless and little regarded. If an upright man of humble parents and a nobleman who has neither decency nor honor come into a country where no one knows them, the son of the commoner will be considered better than the nobleman who has chosen shame rather than esteem. My son, if you want to be a true nobleman, I counsel you to act nobly, for good breeding is surely the highest nobility. You can accept this as the truth."

"Father, you are right," answered the son, "but my cap, hair, and fine clothing won't let me remain here. They are so splendid that they are more suited to a courtly dance than a harrow or plow."

"Oh that you were ever born! You would rather do evil than good. Tell me this, handsome youth, if you have any sense left, who has the better life: the one who is reproached and cursed, who causes everybody suffering because he lives at others' expense and who disdains God's grace, or he from whom all people benefit and who doesn't mind striving night and day to be useful to others and thereby honor God? It seems to me that the latter would please God and man wherever he went, but whom would you like better? Tell me the truth, dear son."

"The man who helps people and doesn't harm anyone, father. His life is the better, of course."

"Dear son, you would be this man if you would take my advice. Till the land, and you will indeed be a blessing to many: rich and poor, wolf and eagle, and all other creatures on earth to which God has given life. Till the land: the produce makes many women beautiful and crowns many kings, for nobody ever became so great but that his splendor depended on farming alone."

"May God quickly spare me your sermon, father! If you had become a real preacher, your exhortations would have sent an entire army on a crusade. Listen to what I say: the more the peasants raise, the more they eat. Whatever happens to me, from now on I'll have nothing to do with a plow. By God, I would never get over the disgrace if I were to have dirty hands from plowing when I dance with the ladies."

"If you don't find it unpleasant," said the father, "ask such wise men as you encounter the meaning of a dream I had. You were holding two candles which burned so brightly that they lit up everything around. My dear son, last year I dreamed this about a man who is now blind."

"You need not say any more, father, for I'll never change my mind because of a tale like that. I would be a coward to do so."

Since this warning did no good, the father continued. "I had another dream. You were walking with one foot on the ground and with the knee of the other leg resting on a piece of wood. What looked like the stump of a leg stuck out from under your coat. If the dream is to be useful to you, you must ask its meaning of those who know."

"It foretells health, good fortune, and joys of all kinds."

"Son, I had a third dream which I'll tell you. Just when you were about to fly high over the forest, one of your wings was cut off and there was no flight. Can this dream bode anything good? Oh your poor hands and feet and eyes!"

"All your dreams predict good fortune for me," said young Helmbrecht. "Now get yourself another farm hand, for you will have to do without me no matter how much you dream."

"The dreams I have told you thus far are nothing compared to this last one. Listen to it. You were up in a tree (it was about one and a half fathoms from your feet to the ground) and a crow and a raven were sitting on a branch above your head. Your hair was unkempt. The raven was combing it on the right side, and the crow was parting it on the left. Oh son, what a dream! Oh the tree, the raven, and the crow! If the dream was no lie, I fear I shall suffer great sorrow for not having raised you better."

"Father, if you dreamed of everything in the world, evil and good, God knows I would not give up my plan until I died. I need to leave more than ever. May God protect you and my dear mother and bless your children. May God keep us all in His care." He thus took leave of his father, trotted past the gate, and rode away. I couldn't tell all about his experiences in three days, perhaps not even in a week.

At last he came to a castle the lord of which was always feuding and was therefore glad to harbor those who were not afraid to ride out and fight with his enemies. The youth joined his troop and became such a zealous robber that he would put in his sack even things that others had let lie. He took everything: no booty was too small or too great. Whether it was rough or smooth, crooked or straight, Farmer Helmbrecht's son seized it. He took the horse and cow and left nothing behind that was worth as much as a spoon. He took jerkin and sword, coat and mantle, nanny goat and billy goat, ewe and ram—but later he paid for them with his own skin. He pulled blouses and skirts off of the women as well as their cloaks and fur coats. Afterwards, when the sheriff seized him, he wished that he had not robbed women. You can be sure of this.

In the first year favorable winds murmured in his sails and his ships faired well. Since he always got the best part of the booty, he became arrogant. Then it occurred to him to go back home to visit his family, as people have always done, so he took leave of his lord and his comrades, commending them to God's care.

Now comes an episode that one must by no means overlook. I only wish I could tell you how he was received at home.

Did they go to meet him? They ran, all together, with one crowding ahead of the other. His father and mother dashed toward him faster than they had ever run to save a calf from death. Who would get the reward for the news? They gladly gave the man who brought it a shirt and trousers. Did the milkmaid and the farm hand cry, "Welcome, Helmbrecht?" No, for they were advised not to. They spoke thus: "We bid you a hearty welcome, sir," to which he answered, "Dear *soete kindekin* [sweet children], God *lat* [grant] you eternal happiness." And when his sister ran up and hugged him, he said. "*Gracia vester* [God's grace be with you]." The young people reached the youth first, but the older ones were not far behind. All of them greeted him joyfully. To his father he said, "*Deu sal* [God keep you]" and to his mother, in Bohemian, "*Dobra ytra* [Good morning]." The man and his wife looked at each other.

"Husband, " she said, "we have made a mistake. This is not our child. It is a Bohemian or a Wend."

"It's a Frenchman," replied the father, "certainly not the son whom I commended to God. Yet they are very much alike." Then the youth's sister Gotelind spoke up: "It isn't your child, for he answered me in Latin. He must be a priest."

"Indeed," said the farm hand, "judging from what I heard, he is from North Germany or Brabant. He said, 'Dear *soete kindekin.*' I think he is a North German."

The farmer asked simply: "Are you my son Helmbrecht? I shall believe it if you will speak a single word as we do and as our fathers have done so that I can understand it. You say only, "*Deu sal,*" and I don't know what to make of that. Honor your mother and me by saying something in German and we shall be forever grateful. I'll curry your horse for you, my dear son—I, myself, not the farm hand—and do it so that you will be really pleased."

"Oh, what *snacket ir geburekin* [are you babbling about, little peasant], and that vulgar *wif* [woman]? Indeed, no peasant shall ever *gegripen an* [touch] my *parit* [palfrey] or my handsome *lif* [self]."

This startled the farmer, but he spoke up again: "If you are my son Helmbrecht, I'll boil you a chicken for this evening and roast you a second one. I mean it. However should you be a Bohemian or a Wend and not my son, then go back to the Wends. God knows I have enough to do with my own children, and I don't give even a priest any more than just what is due him. If you aren't my son, you will never wash your hands to eat at my table, even though I might have all the fish in the world. Should you be North German, Flemish, or French, you will need to have something in your pouch, because you will certainly touch nothing of mine even though the night lasts a year. Eat with the noblemen, sir, for I have neither mead nor wine."

Since it was already quite late, the youth thought to himself: "Good God, I'd better tell them who I am, because there is no innkeeper near here to take me in. It wasn't very clever of me to alter my speech. I won't do it anymore." Then he said, "I am he."

"Now tell me, who?" asked the father.

"He whose name is the same as yours."

"And what is it?"

"Helmbrecht. A year ago I was your son and farm hand. That is the truth."

"No!" exclaimed the father.

"But it's true."

"Then tell me the names of my four oxen."

"I can do it quickly, because I once swung my goad over them and took care of them. One is called Uwer, and he is good enough for the fields of any peasant, no matter how able or rich he might be. The name of the second is Raeme: no gentler ox ever wore a yoke. I'll tell you also what the third was called, Erge. It is because I am clever that I can still name them. And if you want to test me further, the fourth was called Sun. If I named them rightly, then reward me by having someone open the gate."

"You don't need to wait longer in front of either the gate or the door," replied the father, "and both rooms and cupboards will be open to you."

I myself have never had such good treatment as the youth got there: curse the luck! While his mother and sister prepared a soft bed for him, his father took the saddle and bridle off of the palfrey and gave it plenty of fodder. As much as I have roamed about, I have never been in a place where I was cared for as he was.

"Run into the bedroom," the mother called to her daughter, "and get a pad and a soft pillow." The latter was placed under his shoulder on a warm bench by the stove, where he waited in great comfort while the meal was prepared.

When the youth awoke and washed his hands, the food was ready. Now hear what was set before him. I'll begin with the first course, which I would be glad to get even if I were a great nobleman. It was made up of finely chopped cabbage with a good piece of meat that was neither too fat nor too lean. Next came a fat, well-aged cheese. Then—listen, for I know all about it—they set a goose in front of the youth. No fatter one was ever broiled on a spit over the fire: no one was annoyed at this, they were glad to do it. The goose was as large and heavy as a bustard. Two chickens followed: one roasted and one boiled, just as the father had promised. A nobleman who was lying on a stand during a hunt would surely like to get such food. Many other kinds of fine dishes, fare that most peasants know nothing about, were placed before the youth.

"If I had wine," said the father, "we would drink it this evening. In its place, dear son, drink the best spring water that ever flowed out of the ground. I don't know of a spring like ours except the one at Wanghausen, and no one can bring it to us here."

When they had finished this most enjoyable meal, the farmer could wait no longer to ask about the court where his son had been. "Tell me what the customs are there," he said, "and then I'll describe to you the courtly behavior I once observed when I was young."

"Tell me about it, father. Afterwards I'll answer all your questions, for I know the new mode of life very well."

"Long ago when I was young, your grandfather Helmbrecht, my father, used to send me to the court with cheese and eggs, as farmers still do. I saw knights there and took note of all their conduct. They were light-hearted and refined, and knew nothing of the meanness so common among men and women today. The knights had certain customs with which they endeared themselves to the ladies. One was called the bohort, so a courtier told me when I asked about it. They galloped about as if they were mad, but later I heard them praised for it. One troop charged the other and each man rode as though he wanted to knock somebody down. Among us peasants nothing ever happened like the things I saw at court.

"After the bohort was over, they passed the time by dancing to a merry song, but soon a minstrel came and began to play a fiddle. Then the ladies stood up (they were a delight to see), and the knights went to them and took them by the hand. It was a wondrous sight as the splendid knights and ladies, squires and maidens, rich and poor danced joyfully. When this ended, a man came and recited the adventures of a certain Ernst. There were many pleasant things to do, and each found the pastime that he liked. Some shot arrows at a target, others took part in a drive for game, still others hunted alone with hounds.

"He who was the least then would be the best today. Yes indeed, how well I once knew what manner of living causes honor and loyalty to flourish, before it was corrupted by evil. At that time the lords would not keep at their courts those deceitful, shameless men who knew how to pervert justice with their cunning. Nowadays the one who can dissemble and deceive is thought wise, and is a respected man at court; sad to say, he has much greater wealth and esteem than the man who lives uprightly and strives for God's favor. I know this much of the old customs. Now, son, be so kind as to tell me about the new ones."

"I'll be glad to. The courtly thing now is: 'Drink, sir, drink! You empty your cup and I'll drain mine. How could life be better?' Let me make this clear: in former times the highly respected men were to be found in the company of beautiful ladies, but now one sees them only where wine is sold. Morning and evening their greatest concern is how they can see to it that the tavern keeper, when the wine runs out, gets more which is just as good, so they can stay in high spirits. Their love letters go like this: 'My sweet barmaid, keep our cups full. Whoever has felt greater longing for a woman than for good wine is a monkey and a fool.' Today a liar is esteemed, deceit is courtly, and the one who can use cunning words to cheat another is considered well-bred. The slanderer is regarded as virtuous. Believe me, the old people who live like you are now cut off from society. Men and women avoid them as they would a hangman and scorn the authority of both emperor and pope."

"God be merciful!" said the old man. "We should never cease to lament to him that evil has become so widespread."

"The old tournaments have disappeared and new ones have been introduced. Formerly the battle cry was: 'Hey, knights, be merry!' Now they shout from dawn till dark: 'Let's hunt for cattle! Away! Away! Stab and slash! Put out his eyes! Cut off this man's foot and that man's hand. Hang him! Catch me a rich man who'll pay us a good hundred pounds.' Father, I could tell you all about the new customs if I wanted to, for I know them well, but I must sleep now. I have ridden far and need to rest tonight." They followed his wishes. There were no sheets in the house, but his sister Gotelind spread a newly washed shift over his bed. He slept until late in the morning.

I'll tell you what the young Helmbrecht did then. Now was the time for him to get out the delightful things that he had brought his father, mother, and sister from the court. You will truly be pleased to learn what they were. He had brought his father as fine a whetstone as any mower ever tied in its case, the best scythe that was ever swung through the grass (what a present that was for a peasant!), an axe such as no smith has forged for a long time, and also a hoe. The youth gave his mother a splendid coat of fox fur that he had taken off of a priest. (I'll be glad to tell you what was stolen or seized by force if I know.) He gave Gotelind a silk hair ribbon that he had taken from a merchant and a gold-studded belt that would have been more suitable for a nobleman's daughter than his sister. For the hired man he had brought peasant shoes that he would not have carried so far or even touched for anyone else, since he was so refined. However, if Helmbrecht had still been his father's farm hand, the other wouldn't have gotten the shoes at all. He gave the milkmaid a kerchief and a red ribbon, both of which she had wanted very much.

[A voice from the audience]: "Now tell us how long the youth stayed at his father's house."

It was really only seven days, but, since he wasn't out plundering, it seemed to him like a year. Then he abruptly took leave of his parents.

"Don't go, dear, good son," said the father. "If you are willing to live on what I can give you until I die, stay here and eat at our table. Give up this courtly life, my son, for it is evil and bitter. I would rather be a peasant than a poor courtier with no income from land who has to ride about early and late at the risk of his life, always with the fear that his enemies will maim or hang him if they capture him."

"Father," replied the youth, "I thank you very much for your hospitality, but it has been more than a week since I have had any wine, and I am therefore fastening my belt at three holes less. The buckle won't be back where it was until I round up some cattle. Some plows will be stopped and their oxen driven away before I rest up and put on weight again. There is a rich man who has offended me more than anyone ever did before: I once saw him ride across my godfather's grain field. If he lives long enough, he will pay dearly for the insult to me. I am greatly provoked that he should thus cause my dear godfather's work to go for nothing, and his cattle, sheep, and swine will run because of it. I know another rich man who has also wronged me—he ate bread on top of fritters—and I'll avenge it or die. There is still a third rich man who has offended me, indeed more than anyone else. Not even a bishop could get me to overlook the pain he caused me."

"What did he do?" asked the father.

"He loosened his belt at the table. Why, I'll take everything of his that I can capture. The oxen that pull his plow and his wagon will help me to get Christmas clothing. No matter how I look at the matter, I really can't see what this stupid fool is thinking of, nor some others either who have caused me great distress. I'd be a coward not to get revenge. Then there is the man who blew the foam off of his beer. If I don't make him suffer for it at once, I truly will not be worthy of the esteem of ladies and not deserve to gird a sword at my side. It will soon be told of Helmbrecht that he emptied a large farm, for , if I don't find the man, I'll at least drive away his cattle."

"I would be very grateful," said the father, "if you would tell me the names of your young companions who have taught you to seize a rich man's property because he ate bread after fritters. I'd like to know their names."

"My two comrades, Lemberslint [Lamb-Devourer] and Slickenwider [Swallow-the-Ram], taught me this," answered the youth. "I'll also name you others who are my teachers: Hellesac, Rütelschrin, Küefraz and Müschenkelch [Hell-Sack, Shake-Open-the-Coffer, Cow-Eater, and Chalice-Crusher]. That makes six. You can see now, father, what sort of young men belong to our troop. There is also my friend Wolvesguome [Wolf-Jaws]: he treats acquaintances and strangers alike. However dear to him his aunts, uncles, and cousins might be, he doesn't leave them, man or woman, a thread of clothing to cover their nakedness, even in freezing weather. My friend Wolvesdrüzzel [Wolf-Throat] can open any lock or iron chest without a key. In one year I counted a hundred large chests whose locks flew open as soon as he came near, and he drove horses, oxen, and cows without number from farmyards, the bars of which moved from their places when he walked up. I have another comrade who has a more distinguished name than any other youth. It is Wolvesdarm [Wolf-Gut] and was given to him by a mighty duchess, the noble and freeborn Narrie von Nonarre. He likes robbing and stealing so much that he never tires of them, winter or summer. He never took a single step from evil toward goodness: evil deeds draw him like a grain field draws crows."

"Tell me, what name do your friends use when they call you?"

"I'll never be ashamed of my name, father. It is Slintezgeu [Swallow-the-Land]

and I am no joy to the peasants who live near me. Their children have to eat water porridge, but that's not all the distress I cause them. I gouge this one's eye out, tie another on an anthill, pull the hair out of that one's beard with tongs, and smoke a fourth in the smokehouse. I tear the scalp off of some, crush the limbs of some, and hang others up by their heels. Whatever the peasants have belongs to me. When the ten of us ride out together, we can defeat twenty men who are waiting for us, even more."

"My dear son, you know those men whom you have named much better than I. Yet, when God himself wants to take charge, a single sheriff can make them go where he commands, however fierce they may be and though there were three times as many of them."

"Even if all kings were to command it, father, I'll never again act as I have done in the past. I have protected you and mother from my companions and have saved you many chickens and geese as well as cattle, cheese, and fodder. I shall not do this any more. You are attacking the honor of fine young men, none of whom ever does anything that he shouldn't. They have a right to rob and steal. If you hadn't spoiled matters with your foolish chatter and hadn't spoken so scornfully of us, I would have given your daughter Gotelind to my friend Lemberslint as his wife. Then she would have had the best life that any woman in the world ever had with her husband. Had you not said such bitter things about us, he would have given her a wealth of furs, cloaks, and linen, as good as the clergy's best, and she could have eaten fresh beef every week if she had wanted it." [The father and mother go off, and the youth is alone with his sister.]

"Now listen, sister Gotelind. When my friend Lemberslint first asked me for your hand, I said at once: 'Believe me, if you and she are destined to marry, you will never regret it. I know her to be very loyal, and you need have no fear that you may perhaps hang a long time on the gallows. She will cut you down with her own hands and take you to your grave at the crossroads. Then she will carry incense and myrrh around the grave every night for a whole year. You can count on it; the fine and noble lady will fumigate your bones. And if you have the good fortune to be blinded [instead of hung], she will take you by the hand and lead you through all the lands. Should they cut off one of your feet, she will bring your crutches to your bed every morning; and you need not worry if you also lose a hand as punishment, for she will cut your meat and bread for you the rest of your life.'

"To this Lemberslint replied: 'Should your sister Gotelind accept me, I will give her a wedding present that will enable her to live very well. I have three full sacks that are as heavy as lead. One is filled with fine, uncut linen of a quality that would be worth fifteen kreutzers a yard if one wanted to buy it. She will praise this gift. In the second sack are many veils, skirts, and shifts. She will not be poor if she becomes my wife, for I shall give her all this on the day after the wedding and also whatever booty I take from then on. The third sack is stuffed full of costly cloth and many-colored furs, two of which are lined with fine wool. One fur is sable. I have hidden the sacks in a ravine nearby and will give them to her that morning.'

"May God preserve you Gotelind, for your father has spoiled this. Your life will be bitter. No woman ever suffered more grief than you will feel now when you marry a peasant. With him you will have to crush, beat, and scrape the flax and trench the turnips, from all of which the faithful Lemberslint could have saved you. Oh, sister Gotelind, it will pain me if you should have to sleep night after night with a rude peasant whose caresses repel you. One should cry out against your father—he is not my father indeed. I tell you truly that a well-bred courtier came secretly to mother when she had carried me fifteen weeks. I have inherited his traits and those of my godfather. God bless them! Because of them I have always had a noble spirit."

"I don't think I am really his child either," said Gotelind, "for a stately knight lay with mother while she bore me in her womb. He seized her late one evening when she was in the woods looking for the calves. That is why I am so refined. Dear brother Slintezgeu," she continued, "God will reward you if you see to it that Lemberslint becomes my husband. Then my frying pan will sizzle, my cupboards be filled, my beer brewed, my grain finely ground, and grapes be gathered for my wine. Once I get the three sacks, I shall be free of want and have plenty to eat and to wear. Look, what could displease me then? I'll have everything a woman wants from her husband.

"I also expect to give him all a man would like to get from a strong woman like me. I have everything he wants. Father has been making me wait even though I am three times as strong as my sister was when she got married. She could walk without a crutch the next morning and didn't die from the pain. I don't think I shall die of it either unless some calamity occurs. Dear brother, please don't repeat what I am about to say: I'll go with you along the narrow road to the pine forest and become his wife, although—as you know—it may cost me father, mother, and all my kinfolk."

Neither of the parents learned of this decision, and her brother quickly agreed that she should follow him. "I will marry you to this man," he said, "no matter how much it displeases your father. You will become Lemberslint's wife and gain both esteem and wealth thereby. If your mind is made up, I will send a messenger who will lead you to us. Since you two love each other, everything will go well with you. I shall arrange your wedding and see to it that many doublets and robes are given away in your honor: you may depend on it. Get ready sister, and Lemberslint will do the same. I must go now, good-bye. I feel toward father as he does toward me. Farewell, mother."

The youth went back the way he had come and told his friend of Gotelind's assent. Overjoyed, Lemberslint kissed his hand and his clothing all around, then bowed toward the wind that was blowing from the direction of Gotelind.

Now hear what crimes were committed. Many widows and orphans were robbed of their possessions and left in distress before the valiant Lemberslint and his wife sat down on the bridal seat, for plunder was gathered from all around to supply them with food and drink. The young men were by no means idle at this time. Early and late, in wagons and on the backs of horses, they brought everything to the house of Lemberslint's father. When King Arthur married Lady Guinevere, the wedding celebration was nothing compared to that of Lemberslint: these people didn't live on air. As soon as all was ready, Helmbrecht sent the messenger, who soon brought his sister to him. On hearing that Gotelind had arrived, Lemberslint hurried to meet her. Just listen to how he received her!

"Welcome, Lady Gotelind," he said.

"I thank you, Sir Lemberslint," she replied, and many loving glances passed back and forth between them. With refined and courtly words Lemberslint shot his arrow at Gotelind, and she paid him back with woman's speech as well as she could.

Now let us give Gotelind to Lemberslint to be his wife and Lemberslint to Gotelind to be her husband. An old man who could talk well and knew the ceremony stood up, placed them both in a ring, and spoke to Lemberslint: "If you will take Gotelind as your lawful wife, say 'yes.' "

"Yes," said the youth at once. The man asked him again, and he again replied, "Yes." Then he spoke a third time: "Do you take her willingly?" and the youth declared, "By my soul and body, I shall be glad to have this woman." Thereupon the man asked Gotelind, "Do you willingly take Lemberslint to be your husband?"

"Yes, sir, if God will let me have him."

"Do you take him willingly?" he repeated.

"Willingly, sir, give him to me."

"Will you take him?" he asked a third time.

"Gladly, sir, now give him to me." Then Gotelind was given to Lemberslint as his wife, and Lemberslint to Gotelind as her husband. At once all began to sing, and the groom stepped on his bride's foot [a marriage rite].

Since the meal is now ready, we must not forget to supply the bridal couple with court officials. Slintezgeu was the marshal and saw to it that the horses had plenty to eat; Slickenwider was the cupbearer; and Hellesac served as the lord high steward who directed local guests and strangers to their places. The unreliable Rütelschrin was chamberlain; Küefraz was chef and dispensed everything boiled and baked that came from the kitchen; Müschenkelch gave out the bread. It was no modest wedding feast. Wolvesguome, Wolvesdarm, and Wolvesdrüzzel emptied many dishes and large beakers there. The food vanished in front of these young men as if a wind had suddenly swept it away from the table. I know that each of them devoured all the food that the lord high steward brought him from the kitchen. Could a dog have gnawed anything from the bones they discarded? I doubt it, for, as a wise man has said, "everyone is ravenous when his end approaches." The reason they ate so greedily is that they were never again to sit down happily together to eat.

Then the bride spoke up: "Oh! Dear Lemberslint, I am frightened. I am afraid that there are strangers near who intend to harm us. Oh! Father and mother, why am I so far away from you! I greatly fear that Lemberslint's three sacks will bring me pain and disgrace. My heart is so heavy. If only I were at home! I would much rather endure my father's poverty than this anxiety. I have always heard people say that he who wants too much gets nothing at all. Greed hurls us into the depths of hell, for it is a sin, and I have come to my senses too late. Oh, why was I in such haste to follow my brother here? I shall have to suffer for it." Indeed it was soon clear to Gotelind that she would have been better off eating cabbage at her father's table than eating fish with Lemberslint.

They had sat for a while after the meal, and the bride and groom had paid the minstrels, when suddenly they saw five men coming, one a sheriff, who defeated the ten robbers without a struggle. Each crowded ahead of the other as they tried to escape by hiding in the oven or slipping under benches. He who formerly would not have run from four enemies was now pulled forth by the hair by the sheriff's helper alone. I tell you truly that a real thief, however bold he may be and even if he has killed three men at one time, can never defend himself against a sheriff. This one therefore bound the robbers at once with strong ropes. Gotelind lost her wedding dress. Later she was found behind a hedge in a wretched state, holding her hands over her breasts. She had been badly frightened: let him who was there say if anything else had happened to her.

God works miracles, as you can see in this story. A thief who could defeat an army by himself cannot resist a sheriff. When he sees one, even far off, his sight becomes dim and his color pale. He may have been brave and strong before, but a lame sheriff can capture him now. His boldness and cunning vanish as soon as God decides to punish him.

Now listen to the account of the sentencing, of how the thieves, carrying heavy burdens, crept before the court of justice and were hanged. Gotelind was grief-stricken when two cowhides were quickly tied about Lemberslint's neck, but his load was the lightest because he was the bridegroom. The others had to carry more. His brother-in-law Helmbrecht Slintezgeu walked before the sheriff bearing three rawhides, and this was just. Each carried his burden, which became the portion of the judge. They were given no lawyer. May God shorten the life of anyone who wants to lengthen theirs! That is my wish. I know a judge whose nature is such that for pay he would spare a fierce wolf even if it attacked everyone's cattle. This is really true, although it should never be done.

The sheriff then hanged nine of the prisoners and let one live—he had the right to do as he wished with the tenth—and this was Helmbrecht Slintezgeu: what is destined will be. God never overlooks the man whose deeds are evil, as can be seen in the case of Helmbrecht. He was punished for the offense to his father when the sheriff put out his eyes, but that was not the whole penalty: the offense to his mother cost him a hand and foot. He suffered this shame and distress because he had not greeted them with respect. He had said to the one: "What are you babbling about, little peasant?" and had called the other a "vulgar woman." For this sin he had to endure such torment that he would a thousand times rather have died than to live on so miserably.

With grief and remorse the blind thief Helmbrecht parted from Gotelind at a crossroad, as a boy and a crutch brought him home to his father's house. However the father did not give him shelter and help him in his great trouble, but drove him away. Listen to what he said: "*Deu sal*, Sir Blind Man, I learned this greeting long ago at the court. Just go on, little Sir Blind Man. I am sure that you have all that a young nobleman wants: you will be esteemed even in France. I say this because I greet all blind young men thus, but why should I speak further? By God, you will leave my house at once, Sir Blind Youth, and if you don't hurry, I'll have my farm hand give you a beating such as no blind person ever got before. Any bread that I wasted on you this evening would be cursed. Get out."

"Oh no, sir! Let me spend the night here," replied the blind man. "I want to tell you who I am. For God's sake, recognize me!"

"Well speak quickly," said the father, "and hurry off, for it is late. Find yourself another host, because you will get nothing from me."

"Sir," he answered with grief and shame, "I am your son."

"Has the youth who called himself Slintezgeu become blind? Why he wasn't afraid of the threats of the sheriff or of all the judges, however many there might be. You were going to eat iron when you were mounted on the horse for which I gave up my cattle. It doesn't trouble me that you are now creeping along as a blind man. What I regret is the loss of the wool cloth and the grain, since I don't have enough bread myself. I wouldn't give you a crumb if you were at the point of death, so be on your way at once and don't ever come back."

"Since you will no longer accept me as your child," said the blind man, "for God's sake overcome the devil and let me enter your house as a beggar. In Christian charity grant me what you would give another who was sick and destitute. The people of the region hate me, just as you do now, and I shall die if you are not merciful."

The farmer laughed scornfully, but he was sick at heart, for the other was still his own flesh and blood even though he stood blinded before him. "You rode willfully through the world: your horse never ambled, but always went at a trot or a gallop. You were so inhuman that many peasant men and women lost everything because of you. Now tell me if the three dreams haven't come true. But there is more to be told, and things will go still worse for you. Just leave my door quickly before the fourth dream is fulfilled. I would sooner care for a complete stranger the rest of my life than give you half a loaf of bread. Farm hand, bar the door. I want to get some rest tonight."

He thus reproached the blind man for all he had done. The sight of him was a nightmare to the farmer. "Boy," he cried, "lead this hideous creature away from me. This is for you," and he struck the boy. "I would do the same to your master, but I am ashamed to strike a blind man. I am well-bred enough to keep from it, still that can change. Be off at once, you treacherous Russian. I care nothing for your distress." The youth's mother, however, put some bread in his hand, as if he were a child.

The blind thief went on his way. Whenever he passed a field, the peasants would shout at him and the boy: "Hey there, Thief Helmbrecht! If you had tilled the soil as I do, you wouldn't be led around as a blind man." He lived a year thus in misery before he was hanged.

I'll tell you how it happened. Early one morning he was going through a forest seeking food when Helmbrecht was seen by a peasant (who was chopping wood, as peasants do) from whom he once had taken a cow that had calved seven times. As soon as the peasant recognized the blind man, he asked his friends if they would help him.

"Truly," said one, "if no one stops me, I'll tear him to bits. He pulled the clothes right off of my wife and me. I have a just claim to him."

"If there were three of him," exclaimed another, "I would kill them by myself. The rogue broke open my storeroom and took everything I had there."

The fourth of the woodcutters trembled like a leaf with desire. "I'll wring his neck as if he were a chicken," he cried, "and I have a right to. While my child was asleep, he rolled it up with the bedding and shoved it into a sack. This was at night. When it woke up and cried, he shook it out into the snow. It would have died if I had not come to rescue it."

"How pleased I am that he has come," the fifth spoke up, "for today he shall provide me with a sight to delight my heart. He raped my daughter, and I would hang him from a limb even though he were three times as blind. I myself lost everything, even my clothes, and barely escaped from him with my life. Now that he has crept into this deep forest, I would get vengeance if he were as large as a house."

"At him!" they shouted then, and all of them rushed at Helmbrecht. While they avenged themselves with blows, they cried, "Watch out for your cap, Helmbrecht!" The part of it that the sheriff's helper had left unharmed was now ripped to bits. It was horrible: there wasn't a piece left the size of a penny. The parrots and larks, falcons and turtledoves which were embroidered on the cap were strewn on the road. Here lay a lock of hair, there a shred of cloth. If I ever told you the truth, you must believe what I say about the cap and the tiny scraps into which they tore it. You never saw a head so bald, since all of Helmbrecht's curly, blond hair lay in the dirt. However, this was the least of his troubles.

After they had heard the wretch make his confession, one of the peasants picked up a fragment of soil and placed it in the mouth of the sinner as a wafer to help him against hell's fire. Then they hanged him from a tree, and the prophesy of the father's dream thus proved to be true. Here the story ends.

Let this be a warning to other children who will not listen to their father and mother. If they act like Helmbrecht, I can safely predict that they will end as he did. He is still hanging by a willow withe, and the wagon traffic that had disappeared from the roads and highways is moving peacefully again. Now give heed and follow good advice whether it comes from an unlettered man or a sage. I wonder if there are still some young admirers of Helmbrecht about? Should there be, they will become little Helmbrechts, and I shall give you no peace until I have brought them also to the gallows.

Pray that God may be merciful to him who reads you this story and to the poet, Wernher the Gardener.

Notes

[1]Some scholars have suggested that the source to which Hartmann refers was a lost history of his liege lord's family or possibly even of his own family. A better case can be made for a medieval sermon parable (extant in two Latin versions) that is certainly related to *Poor Heinrich*, but is probably not as old. Estelle Morgan, "A Source for *Der arme Heinrich?*" *Notes and Queries*, n.s. 11 (1964): 209-10, thinks Hartmann may have drawn from the life of the leper Margrave Otokar IV of Traungau, and Friedrich Weller, "Der arme Heinrich in Indien," *Orientalische Literaturzeitung* 68 (1973): 437-48, points to an oriental tale as a possible source. An account of the healing of William the Conqueror's son, Duke Robert of Normandy, in Salerno and the legend of Lady Godiva have also been mentioned as having possibly contributed to Hartmann's work.

[2]Such a heroine also appears in the episode of the *Queste del Saint Graal* (ca. 1225) in which a leprous woman is told by a wise man that she can be cured by washing in the blood of a virgin. Perceval's sister gives her blood to heal the woman and dies as a result.

[3]The most controversial question that has been raised with respect to *Poor Heinrich* has to do with the guilt or innocence of the hero. Although differing from one another in detail, the many answers that have been advanced fall into three main groups with the following interpretations: (1) Heinrich is from the beginning guilty of inordinate pride, as he himself confesses, (2) he is originally innocent but later sins by being unwilling to accept God's chastisement and/or by agreeing to let the girl die for him, (3) he does not sin at all since at the crucial moment he does pass the test. The various theories are sketched briefly by Günther Datz in *Die Gestalt Hiobs in der kirchlichen Exegese und der "Arme Heinrich" Hartmanns von Aue*, Göppinger Arbeiten zur Germanistik, no. 108 (Göppingen: Kümmerle, 1973, pp. 203-208.

[4]Bert Nagel, *Der arme Heinrich Hartmanns von Aue: Eine Interpretation* (Tübingen: Niemeyer, 1952), pp. 51-56, represents those who regard the hero's decision here as the last step in a long, gradual process of atonement and regeneration. His arguments are opposed by Timothy Buck, among others, in "Heinrich's Metanoia: Intention and Practice in *Der arme Heinrich*," *Modern Language Review* 60 (1965): 391-4, where he speaks of the sudden transformation of the hero's whole being as a result of a moment of true insight. Nagel believes that the girl's beauty affected Heinrich only as a symbol of her inner self, while Helmut de Boor, *Hartmann von Aue: Der arme Heinrich: Mittelhochdeutscher Text und Übertragung* (Frankfurt: Fischer, 1967), p. 124, considers it an emblem of the physical loveliness of this world and the decisive factor in Heinrich's resignation to God's will: the girl is simply too beautiful to die. Eva-Maria Carne, *Die Frauengestalten*

bei Hartmann von Aue (Marburg: Elwert, 1970), p. 118, maintains that the chief effect of her beauty was to cause Heinrich to realize the depth of his affection for the girl. Other interpreters see the naked figure as a Christ Symbol.

[5]Contemporary evaluations of the girl figure vary greatly. Ronald Finch, "Guilt and Innocence in Hartmann's *Der arme Heinrich,*" *Neuphilologische Mitteilungen* 73 (1972): 646, presents the older point of view when he maintains that her sole consideration is to restore Heinrich to health. Timothy Buck, "Hartman's 'reine maget,' " *German Life and Letters* 18 (1965): 175, views the girl as only an agent and states that her extreme fervor is necessary to make her sacrifice plausible. Rolf Endres, "Über die gesellschaftliche Bedingtheit psychologischer Strukturen in der mittelhochdeutschen Literatur," *Zeitschrift für Literaturwissenschaft und Linguistik* 3, 11 (1973), 71-79, postulates sociological and psychological conditions that caused her to assume the role of a martyr. A survey of further speculation concerning the girl appears in William C. McDonald, "The Maiden in Hartmann's *Armen Heinrich*: Enite redux?" *Deutsche Vierteljahrsschrift für Literaturwissenschaft und Geistesgeschichte* 53 (1979): 34-48.

[6]Discussions of fairy tale material in *Poor Heinrich* appear in Gerhard Eis, "Salernitanisches und Unsalernitanisches im 'Armen Heinrich' des Hartmann von Aue," *Forschungen und Fortschritte* 31 (1957): 77-81; Leslie Seiffert, "The Maiden's Heart: Legend and Fairy-tale in Hartmann's *Der arme Heinrich,*" *Deutsche Vierteljahrsschrift für Literaturwissenschaft und Geistesgeschichte* 37 (1963): 384-405; and Theodorus C. van Stockum, "Eine crux philologorum: Die prognostisch-therapeutische Formel im *Armen Heinrich* des Hartmann von Aue," *Neophilologus* 48 (1964): 146-50.

[7]*Hartmann von Aue: Der arme Heinrich*, 14th ed. (Tübingen: Niemeyer, 1972).

[8]Ruth Harvey, *Moriz von Craûn and the Chivalric World* (Oxford: Clarendon, 1961), pp. 297-305, presents linguistic evidence for locating the work in the Strasbourg-Worms region and cites various scholars on the subject. Günther J. Gerlitzke, *Die Bedeutung der Minne in "Moriz von Craûn"* (Bern: Lang, 1970), p. 23, gives a broad sampling of scholarly opinions on the date of composition. To his list should be added the important concession by A. T. Hatto, "Moriz von Craon," *London Medieval Studies* 1 (1938): 300, that the story might have been composed as late as the mid-thirteenth century.

Although it is commonly assumed that the primary source of *Moriz* was a lost French work, there is wide disagreement as to the extent to which the German novella followed it. Kurt Ruh, "Moriz von Craûn: Eine höfische Thesenerzählung aus Frankreich," *Formen mittelalterlicher Literatur*, ed. Otmar Werber et al. (Göppingen: Kümmerle, 1970, pp. 77-90, attempts to prove that nothing was added or altered by the German poet. Most scholars, however, believe him responsible for the introduction and perhaps much more. It is likely that the nucleus of the story was supplied by the fabliau, "Du chevalier qui recovra l'amor de sa dame," which has the closest resemblance to *Moriz* of any extant work. The Oriental tales suggested as possible sources by Franz Rolf Schröder, "Zum Moriz von Craûn," *Germanisch-Romanische Monatsschrift* 35 (1954): 337-40 are less similar.

[9]Historical data on members of the Craon and Beaumont families are given by Harvey, *Moriz von Craûn*, pp. 49-53, and Karl Heinz Borck, "Zur Deutung und Vorgeschichte des *Moriz von Craûn,*" *Deutsche Vierteljahrsschrift für Literaturwissenschaft und Geistes-*

geschichte 35 (1961): 494-520. Borck, p. 506, suggests political reasons for linking Maurice and Richard to the story.

[10]Perhaps the most significant of the many interpretations of *Moriz* are those by Heimo Reinitzer, "Zu den Tiervergleichen und zur Interpretation des Moriz von Craûn," *Germanisch-Romanische Monatsschrift* 58 (1977): 1-18, who regards the work as a serious satire of the concept of courtly love, and Heinrich Meyer, "Mauritius am Scheideweg," in Gerlitzki, *Die Bedeutung der Minne*, pp. 115-131, who sees it as pure humor.

[11]The more obvious literary sources for the historical introduction are briefly discussed in R. Folz, "L'Historie de la chevalerie d'après *Moriz von Craûn*," *Etudes Germaniques* 32 (1977), 119-128.

[12]A brief report on medieval accounts of ships on wheels appears in Lothar George Seeger, "The Middle High German Epic *Moriz von Craon* and the New Morality," *Susquehanna University Studies* 8 (1970): 263-64.

[13]The symbolism of wondrous beds in medieval German literature is discussed in Heimo Reinitzer, "Zeder und Aloe: Zur Herkunft des Bettes Salomos im *Moriz von Craûn*," *Archiv für Kulturgeschichte* 58 (1976): 1-34.

[14]*Moriz von Craûn*, 3d. ed., edited by Ulrich Pretzel et al. (Tübingen: Niemeyer, 1966). An account of the manuscript and earlier editions appears in Karl Stackmann, "Die mittelhochdeutsche Versnovelle *Moriz von Craûn*" (Ph.D. dissertation, University of Hamburg, 1947), pp. 1-10.

[15]Since the superscriptions of the manuscripts name the novella after Emperor Otto instead of Heinrich, to whom the greater space is devoted, there has been considerable discussion as to what the proper title should be and who should be considered the principle figure. This scholarship is examined by Rosemary E. Wallbank, "Emperor Otto and Heinrich von Kempten," *Studies in Medieval Literature and Languages in Memory of Frederick Whitehead*, ed. W. Rothwell et al. (New York: Barnes & Nobel, 1973), pp. 353-62. A general evaluation of Konrad's novellas appears in David M. Blamires, "Konrad von Würzburg's Verse *Novellen*," *Medieval Miscellany Presented to Eugène Vinaver*, ed. F. Whitehead et al. (Manchester: University Press, 1965), pp. 28-44.

[16]The other extant versions are printed in *Otto mit dem Barte*, ed. Karl August Hahn (Quedlinburg: Basse, 1838; reprint edition, Amsterdam: RODOPI, 1969), pp. 22-29.

[17]The fullest treatment of the humor of *Heinrich von Kempten* appears in Stephen L. Wailes, "Konrad von Würzburg and Pseudo-Konrad: Varieties of Humor in the *Märe*," *Modern Language Review* 69 (1974): 103-7. Certain critics view the work as serious, didactic literature. Lutz Röhrich, "*Kaiser Otto oder Heinrich von Kempten*," *Germanisch-Romanische Monatsschrift* 32 (1950-51): 151-54, sees it as a warning against outbreaks of rage and an admonition to self-control, an interpretation that has been ably refuted by Wallbank, "Emperor Otto," pp. 358-60. Hans Joachim Gernentz, "Konrad von Würzburg: Charakter und Bedeutung seiner Dichtung," *Weimarer Beiträge* 7 (1961): 42-43, and Stefan F. L. Grunwald, "Konrad von Würzburg's Realistic Souvereign and Reluctant Servitor," *Mediaeval Studies* 32 (1970): 273-81, consider the novella social criticism, a satire of

knighthood and the nobility. Hubertus Fischer and Paul-Gerhard Völker, "Konrad von Würzburg: *Heinrich von Kempten:* Individuum und feudale Anarchie," *Literatur im Feudalismus,* ed. Dieter Richter (Stuttgart: Metzler, 1975), pp. 83-130), believe the purpose of the work is to illustrate basic problems of feudal society.

[18] *Kleinere Dichtungen Konrads von Würzburg,* vol. 1, 3d ed. (Berlin: Weidmann, 1959). Perhaps the best general survey of Konrad's writings appears in Helmut de Boor, *Das späte Mittelalter: Zerfall und Neubeginn,* pt. 1 (Munich: Beck, 1967), pp. 27-52. A summary of the poet's reputation in the Middle Ages is given in *Konrad von Würzburg: Heinrich von Kempten, Der Welt Lohn, Das Herzmaere,* ed. and tr. Heinz Rölleke (Stuttgart: Reclam, 1968), pp. 146-47, 152-53.

[19] The dates cited apply to the novella as we know it. An oral version, perhaps dealing only with the rose garden episode, might have been much older. Among those who assume the existence of such a Laurin story are Carl Brestowsky, *Der Rosengarten zu Worms* (Stuttgart: Kohlhammer, 1929), p. 77, and Hellmut Rosenfeld, "König Laurin," *Die deutsche Literatur des Mittelalters: Verfasserlexikon,* vol. 5 (Berlin: De Gruyter, 1955), p. 530. However, Jan de Vries, "Bemerkungen zur Laurin-dichtung," Beiträge zur Geschichte der deutschen Sprache und Literatur 56 (1932): 178-79, maintains that the written version had no specific legendary antecedent.

[20] Ilsung is perhaps the warrior monk Ilsan of the medieval narrative *Der Rosengarten zu Worms,* in which Dietrich and his companions reappear. Some scholars have attempted to learn something of the Laurin figure from the etymology of the name. Justus Lunzer, "Rosengartenmotive," *Beiträge zur Geschichte der deutschen Sprache und Literatur* 50 (1926): 212, postulates an Old Ladin word *laurein,* meaning "stone land," and assumes that it was a Tirolean place name which was given to the dwarf by the author of the novella. Otto Luitpold Jiriczek, *Deutsche Heldensage,* vol. 1 (Strassburg: Trübner, 1898), p. 251, is one of several who derive the name from Middle High German *lûr* or *lûre,* with the meaning "kobold," and suppose that the figure was already connected with a rose garden legend before the novella was composed. Eberhard Klaass, "König Laurin," *Die deutsche Literatur des Mittelalters: Verfasserlexikon,* vol. 2 (Berlin: De Gruyter, 1936), p. 844, cites Georg Panzer as identifying Laurin with a historical Count Lorenz of Tirol.

[21] Hermann Schneider, *Germanische Heldensage,* vol. 1 (Berlin: De Gruyter, 1928), p. 268; Torsten Dahlberg, *Zwei unberücksichtigte mittelhochdeutsche Laurin-Versionen* (Lund: Ohlsson, 1948), p. 12; and others criticize the novella as lacking unity, the result of loosely tying together two unrelated themes: the defense of the rose garden and the kidnaping of a maiden. In rebuttal one can say that the events in the mountain have little to do with the freeing of Kühnhilde, but grow out of Laurin's need to avenge his defeat.

[22] Helmut de Boor, *Das späte Mittelalter: Zerfall und Neubeginn,* pt. 1 (Munich: Beck, 1967), p. 168, discusses the work also in terms of a demonic-courtly polarity.

[23] Extensive treatment of sources and analogues to *Laurin* is found in Karl Felix Wolff, *König Laurin und sein Rosengarten* (Bozen: Athesia, 1947) and P. B. Wessels, "König Laurin, Quelle und Struktur," *Beiträge zur Geschichte der deutschen Sprache und Literatur* (Tübingen) 84 (1962): 245-65.

[24]The Low German, Danish, and Faroese versions are examined by Jan de Vries, "Bemerkungen;" Stanislaw Sawicki, "Zum dänischen Laurin," *Arkiv för nordisk Filologe* 56 (1941): 267-74; and Torsten Dahlberg, *Zum dänischen Lavrin und niederdeutschen Lorin* (Lund: Gleerup, 1950) and "Laurinprobleme," *Niederdeutsche Mitteilungen* 8 (1952): 46-53. The influence and popularity of the High German version is treated especially by Karl Wolff, *König Laurin*, pp. 198-215, who lists many of the modern works that have treated the Laurin material. An account of the mural is given by Karl Müllenhoff, "Zeugnisse und Excurse zur deutschen Heldensage," *Zeitschrift für deutsches Altertum und deutsche Literatur* 12 (1865): 425-27.

[25]*Laurin: Ein tirolisches Heldenmärchen aus dem Anfange des XIII. Jahrhunderts*, 5th ed. (Berlin: Weidmann, 1926; reprint ed., Hamburg: Hansischer Gildenverlag, 1948). This text differs from one by Georg Holz, *Laurin und der kleine Rosengarten*(Halle: Niemeyer, 1897), in that the latter ends the story proper with Laurin a prisoner and object of ridicule at the Veronese court and presents the reconciliation between Dietrich and the dwarf only as a continuation by a later poet. The medieval audience would have expected the conciliatory ending of Müllenhoff's edition because of the parallel plot structure of the novella and also because of the manner in which Laurin is portrayed before his captivity, for he is depicted neither as a potentially tragic nor potentially comic character. Contrary to Holz, p. XVI, he is also not shown to be essentially and incorrigibly evil.

[26]Helmut Brackert, *Helmbrecht: mittelhochdeutscher Text und Übertragung* (Frankfurt: Fischer, 1972), pp. 130-31, and Peter Krahé, "Slintezgeu Helmbrecht," *Euphorion* 73 (1979): 107-8, discuss the separate theories concerning the identity of the poet. Brackert, p. 132, also presents the evidence and the theories with respect to the time of composition. Bruno Steinbruckner, "Dichter und Schauplatz des *Helmbrecht*," *Euphorion* 62 (1968): 378-84, summarizes the various studies of the work's geographical setting.

[27]Fritz Martini, "Der 'Meier Helmbrecht' des Wernher der Gartenaere und das mittelalterliche Bauerntum," *Zeitschrift für Deutschkunde* 51 (1937): 414-26, and Gerhard Schindele, "Helmbrecht: Bäuerlicher Aufstieg und landesherrliche Gewalt," *Literatur im Feudalismus*, ed. Dieter Richter (Stuttgart: Metzler, 1975), pp. 131-211, describe the general historical and cultural background of the novella. Horst Wenzel, " 'Helmbrecht' wider Hapsburg: Das Märe von Wernher dem Gärtner in der Auffassung der Zeitgenossen," *Euphorion* 71 (1977): 230-49, attempts to fit it into a specific historical situation.

[28]Kurt Ruh, "Helmbrecht und Gregorius," *Beiträge zur Geschichte der deutschen Sprache und Literatur* (Tübingen) 85 (1963): 102-6, presents a detailed comparison of the novella with *Gregorius*. Herbert Kolb, "Der 'Meier Helmbrecht' zwischen Epos und Drama," *Zeitschrift für deutsche Philologie* 81 (1962): 1-23, assumes the influence of the Biblical parable of the prodigal's son and suggests that Wernher may have known a dramatization of it. Krahé, "Slintezgeu Helmbrecht," pp. 110-12, and Kurt Ruh, "Einleitung," *Die Märe vom Helmbrecht von Wernher dem Gartenaere*, 6th ed., edited by Friedrich Panzer (Tübingen: Niemeyer, 1960), pp. XIX-XXIII, cite various other studies of Wernher's sources.

[29]Edmund Wiessner, ed., *Die Lieder Neidharts* (Tübingen: Niemeyer, 1955). See especially *Sommerlieder*, nos. 1 and 23 and *Winterlieder*, no. 29.

[30]Further analyses of the structure of *Helmbrecht* are given by Frank G. Banta, "The Arch of Action in *Meier Helmbrecht*," *Journal of English and Germanic Philology* 63 (1964): 696-711; Werner Fechter, "Gliederung thematischer Einheiten, beobachtet an drei mittelhochdeutschen Verserzählungen," *Beiträge zur Geschichte der deutschen Sprache und Literatur* (Tübingen) 87 (1965): 394-405; Ernst von Reusner, "Helmbrecht," *Wirkendes Wort* 22 (1972): 108-22; Werner Brettschneider, *Die Parabel vom verlorenen Sohn: Das biblische Gleichnis in der Entwicklung der europäischen Literatur* (Berlin: Schmidt, 1978), pp. 19-22; and others.

[31]Most *Helmbrecht* criticism idealizes the father. Hermann Bausinger, "Helmbrecht: Eine Interpretationsskizze," *Studien zur deutschen Literatur und Sprache des Mittelalters: Festschrift für Hugo Moser zum 65. Geburtstag*, ed. Werner Besch et al. (Berlin: Schmidt, 1974), 207, identifies the father with God.

[32]The fullest treatments of humor in *Helmbrecht* are by George Nordmeyer, "Structure and Design in Wernher's *Meier Helmbrecht*," *Publications of the Modern Language Association of America* 67 (1952): 259-87, and Bernhard Sowinski, "Helmbrecht der Narr," *Beiträge zur Geschichte der deutschen Sprache und Literatur* (Tübingen) 90 (1968): 223-42.

[33]Scholarship is divided on the question as to whether Wernher was primarily concerned with Helmbrecht's attempt to rise above his station or with his breaking the Fourth Commandment. The former (majority) opinion is supported by W. T. H. Jackson, "The Composition of Meier Helmbrecht," *Modern Language Quarterly* 18 (1957): 44-58, the latter by Hanns Fischer, "Gestaltungsschichten im 'Meier Helmbrecht,' " *Beiträge zur Geschichte der deutschen Sprache und Literatur* 79 (1957): 85-109.

[34]*Meier Helmbrecht von Wernher dem Gartenaere*, 5th ed. (Tübingen: Niemeyer, 1953). The data on the use of *Helmbrecht* by modern writers come from Manfred Lemmer, "Geleitwort," *Wernher der Gärtner: Helmbrecht*, trans. Fritz Bergemann, 3rd ed. (Leipzig: Insel, 1965), p. 71.